WORKS OF ART

JOE CHIODO

HERMES PRESS

NESHANNOCK, PENNSYLVANIA

WORKS OF ART

JOE CHIODO

INTRODUCTION BY DANIEL HERMAN

HERMES
PRESS

NESHANNOCK, PENNSYLVANIA

Published by Hermes Press
2100 Wilmington Road
Neshannock, Pennsylvania 16105
(724) 652-0511
E-mail Geerherm@sgi.net

Cover painting by Joe Chiodo
Book design by Daniel Herman

First printing, May, 2003

All artwork courtesy of, and selected pieces are available for sale by Mitch Itkowitz and Graphic Collectibles, 22 Blue Hills Drive, Saugerties, N.Y. 12477, (845) 246-0952, E-mail mitkowitz@hvc.rr.com, www.graphiccollectibles.com

Library of Congress Control Number: 2003102780

Hardcover signed, limited edition
ISBN 0-9710311-5-0
Hardcover ISBN 0-9710311-9-3
Trade paperback ISBN 0-9710311-8-5

Hardcover dustjacket and hardcover limited edition dustjacket painting, Pleasure and Pain, 2003, acrylic on board
Trade paperback cover painting, Painted Swirls in Blue and Green, 2003, acrylic and oil on board

Proof reading by: Louise Herman, Sabrina Herman, Lori Geramita, Francesca Occhibone, Elaine Devivo, and Stephanie Cooper

Printed in China

DEDICATION

For my family, Lisa, Nina and Anthony

ACKNOWLEDGMENTS

This type of project could not be completed without the help and inspiration of others. I would like to first thank my wife, Lisa, whose unwavering support and encouragement has lifted me through some of the tougher times. Also, for Dan Herman and Mitch Itkowitz who had the difficult task of putting this project together and dealing with me. Also, for Jeff Watts and Eric Gist who have been a great source of inspiration. Finally to Renard Garr for all the coffee, and Bill Sienkiewicz for opening my eyes, many years ago, to color. --Joe Chiodo

WORKS OF ART

JOE CHIODO

TABLE OF CONTENTS

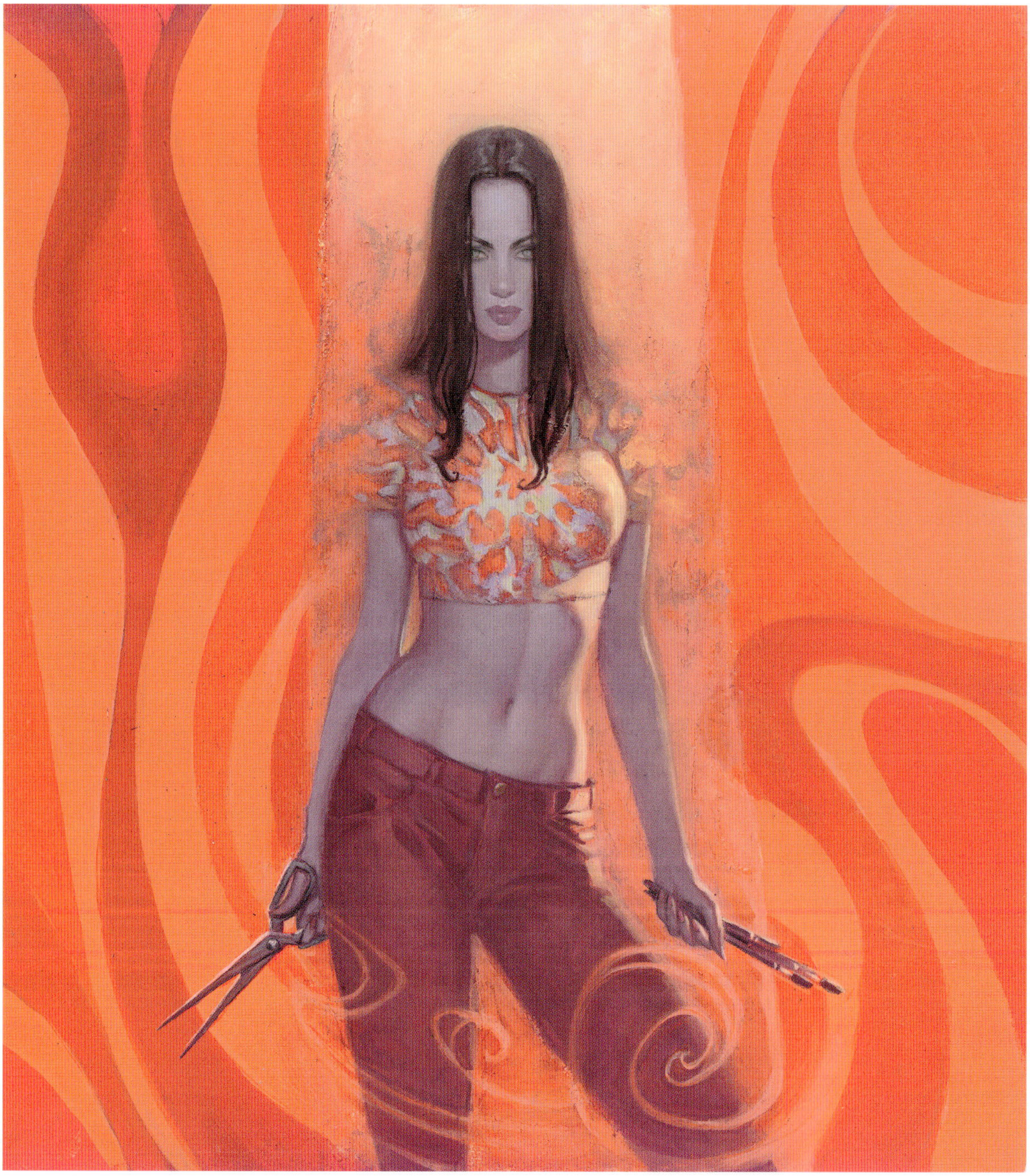

Pleasure and Pain, 2003, acrylic and oil on board

INTRODUCTION
THEN AND NOW

For over twenty years Joe Chiodo has been actively involved in different forms of illustration. He has worked as a cover artist for numerous paperback books and later as a colorist and comic book storyteller known for his painted covers, pin-ups, and stories. For the past two years though, Joe has been out of the public eye, teaching and painting. To show everyone what Joe has been up to, we present *Works of Art*, which not only takes a brief look at Joe's past work, to show you where he has been, but, most importantly, focuses on where he is going with his recent painting. For those familiar with Joe's work, his new paintings and drawings will not come as any great surprise. Joe's work is becoming more assured and mature, without losing its playfulness and sense of whimsy.

To understand the work in this book, it must be viewed in the perspective of illustration and comic book storytelling at the end of the 1970s. Art students and aspiring young illustrators entering the comic book field were trying to integrate painting into their storytelling and into comics in general. Painted comic book covers were nothing new, various publishers had used painted covers since the Golden Age of comics, but painted artwork was used infrequently, with the exception of Western Publishing's pulpy looking Gold Key covers. The stories in comic books had always been pencilled and inked by one team of artists (the division of labor solely to save production time) with the coloring of the artwork being left to a third person, many times with little or no input from the penciler, who conceived the artwork in the first place. Chiodo entered the professional art world in this environment.

Joe Chiodo was born in 1958 in Sharon, Pennsylvania. His family relocated to San Jose, California, where he grew up with the ambition of becoming an artist. In 1979, he made the trek to New York, with fellow artist Brent Anderson, with nothing more than a sleeping bag, his portfolio, and a suitcase, looking for work as an artist. For illustrators and comic book artists, New York City was the center of the universe. All the major comic book and paperback book publishers had offices in the city and artists made the rounds from publisher to publisher, looking for assignments. Chiodo first found work illustrating paperback novel covers and quickly distinguished himself working on a number of assignments. During this period he painted dozens of covers and began to concentrate on developing his "own voice" as an illustrator. He also began to consider the idea of adapting his approach to cover illustration for contemporary comic books.

The 1980s saw a large influx of new talent into the comic book field centered in and around the New York area. Always on the lookout for studio accommodations, Chiodo and Anderson met Bill Sienkiewicz and they talked about sharing studio space. Sienkiewicz's apartment building had a va-

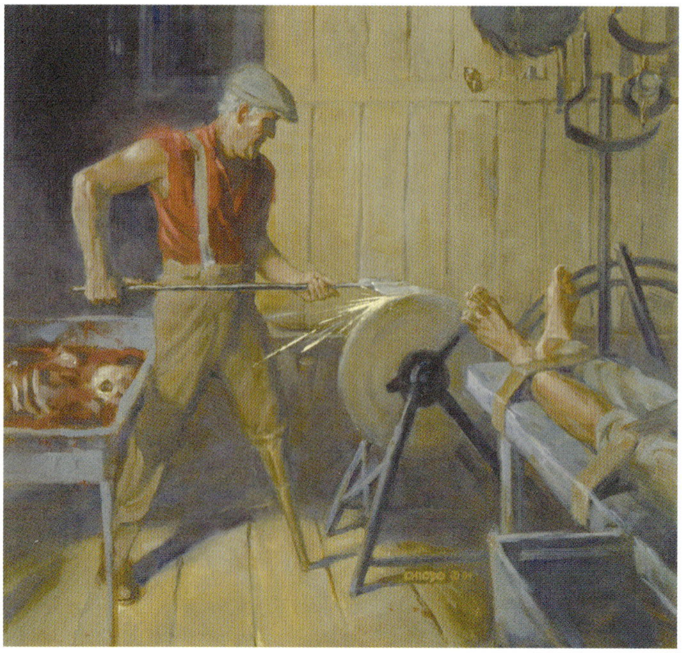

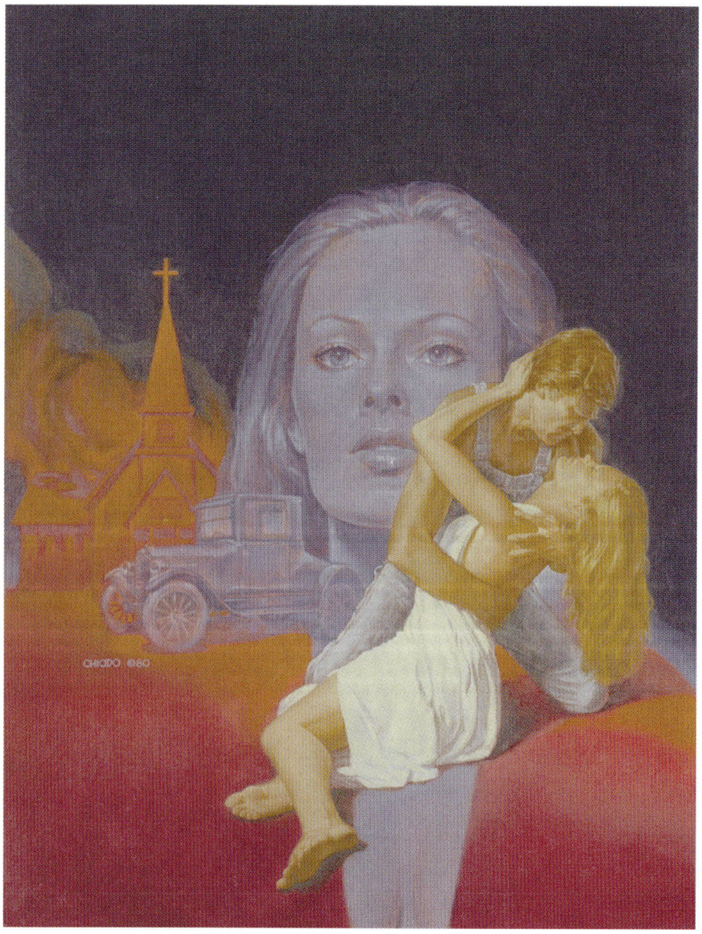

cancy and Chiodo and Anderson relocated to Connecticut renting studio space about a mile away and beginning a small comic artists' colony in the area. Chiodo, Anderson, and Sienkiewicz's group was later joined by Terry Austin and Brett Blevins. By 1981, Chiodo began painting a series of well received comic book covers for Marvel's *Savage Sword of Conan* series, and he was hooked.

Chiodo's work at the time incorporated elements from pulp, science fiction, and fantasy into his artwork. One essential ingredient in pulp magazine and paperback book cover art was the use of enticing and alluring women to beguile potential book buyers into purchasing the book or magazine solely on the basis of the cover. In making the transition from illustration to comics, Chiodo used his experience as an illustrator and brought another well known genre to comic books, "girl art." Chiodo's focus on women however, was entirely different in attitude and emphasis from the infamous (or famous, depending on your perspective) bondage and jungle girl comics from the 1950s. Chiodo, who has a much admired and inimitable style of depicting the female form, offered comic book readers a style which blends the sensibilities of contemporary comic books with the sensuous qualities of pin-up or girl art. The art and attitude of even the less offensive girl art comic books of the 1950s is crude by any comparison. Indeed, Chiodo's work in comic books, posters, and covers have brought girl art into the 21st century by presenting his women in a style that mixes classic good girl painting with comic book design.

During the 1980s, Chiodo was busy working for a host of different publishers

Top: Footloose, 1984, oil on canvas, original cover artwork from *Twisted Tales* #9, November/ 1984, ©2003, Pacific Comics. Below: Burning Love, 1980, oil on canvas, paperback cover art, ©2003 the respective copyright holder.

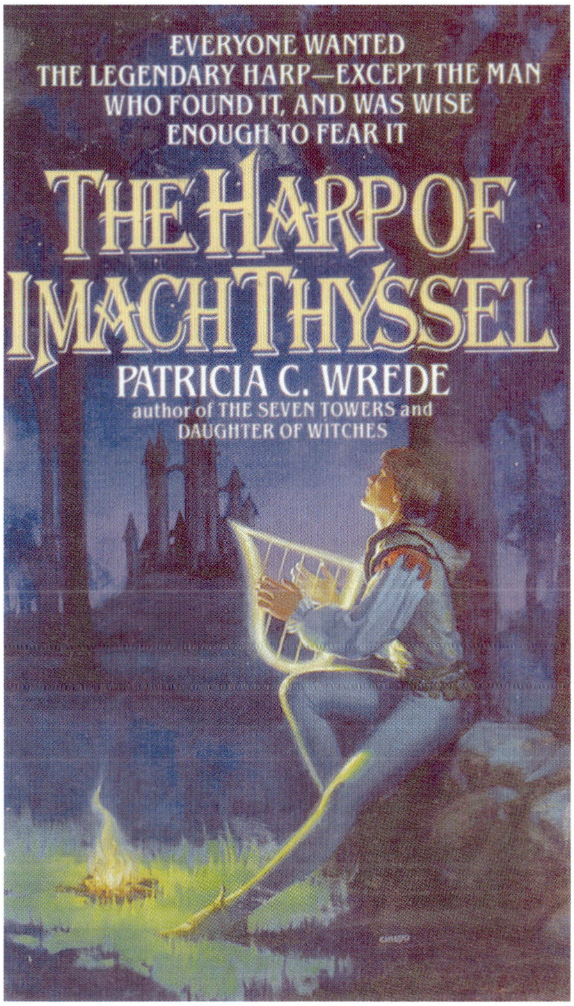

on comic books as an artist, inker, cover illustrator, and colorist. He turned in work on titles ranging from Marvel's *Savage Sword of Conan* (1981-83, cover art), *Power Man and Iron Fist* (1982, inks), *Kull the Conqueror* (1983, inks), and *Moon Night* (1983, inks) to Pacific Comic's *Alien Worlds* (1982-84, cover art and colors), *Somerset Holmes* (1983-84, colors), and *Twisted Tales* (1983-84, cover art and colors) to Eclipse's *Rocketeer* (1985, colors). Chiodo also began his association with one of his favorite comic book characters, Vampirella, by creating the first of many memorable cover illustrations. Chiodo enjoys his opportunities to paint Vampirella because, "she is evil

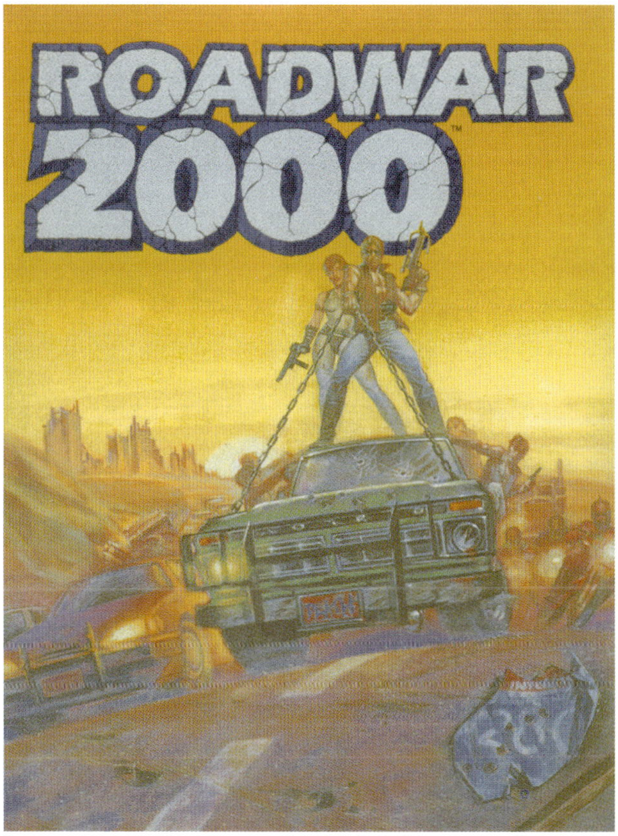

and sultry at the same time." He recalls, "when I had the opportunity to paint some covers, I jumped at the chance."

In 1986, Chiodo also had the opportunity to paint the poster art for the direct-to-video release of the *Day of the Dead*. His artwork was used on posters, promotional art and on the video release cover. After finishing the artwork, Chiodo remembers the art director requesting more detail. Chiodo recalls, "they wanted more detail in the decayed teeth!"

In the 1990s, Chiodo was in constant demand as a comic book artist, cover illustrator and colorist. He was responsible for coloring a majority of the comic books produced by Image which included, *Codename Stryke Force*, *Cyber Force*, *Deathblow*,

Above left: The Harp of Imach Thyssel, 1985, oil on board, ©2003 Ace Fantasy. Right: Roadwar 2000, 1986, acrylic on board, ©2003 Strategic Simulations, Inc.

Left: Alien Worlds, 1982, acrylic on board, *Alien Worlds* #1, December/1982, ©2003 Pacific Comics/Eclipse. Right: Leather and Lace, 1998, acrylic on board, *Leather and Lace II*, 1998, ©2003 Sal Q.

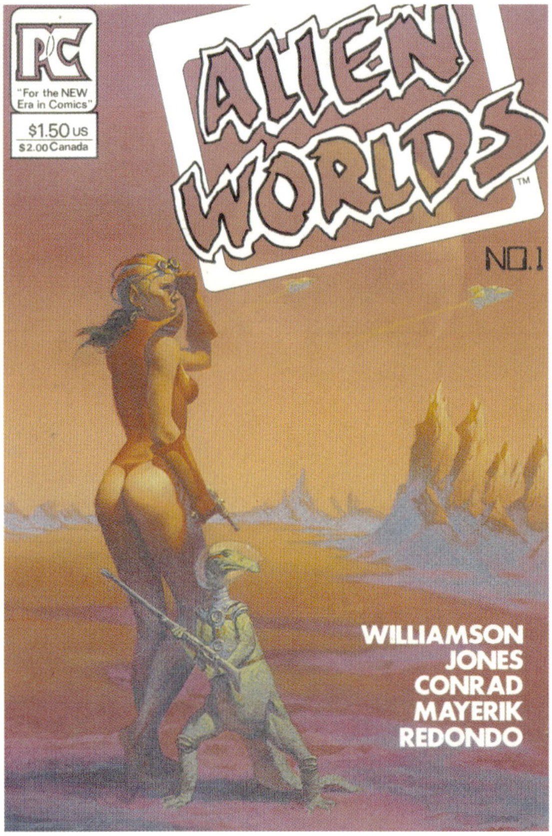

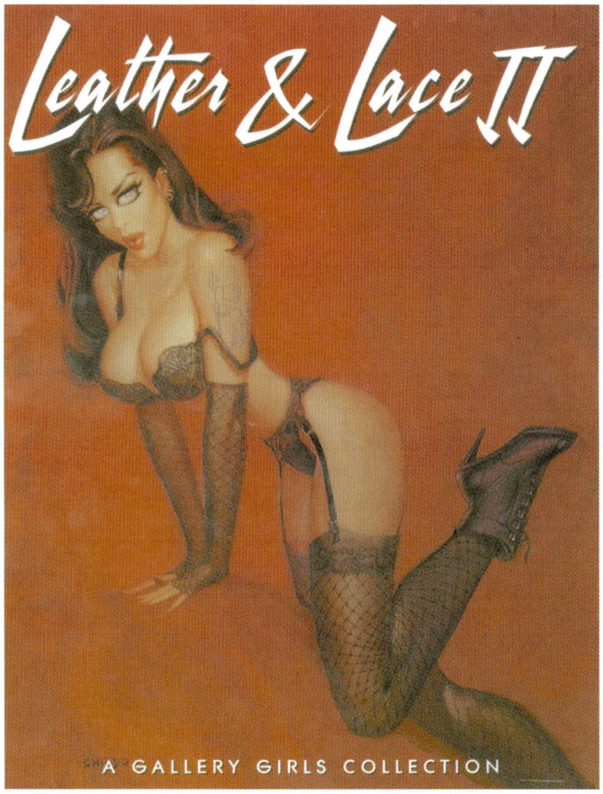

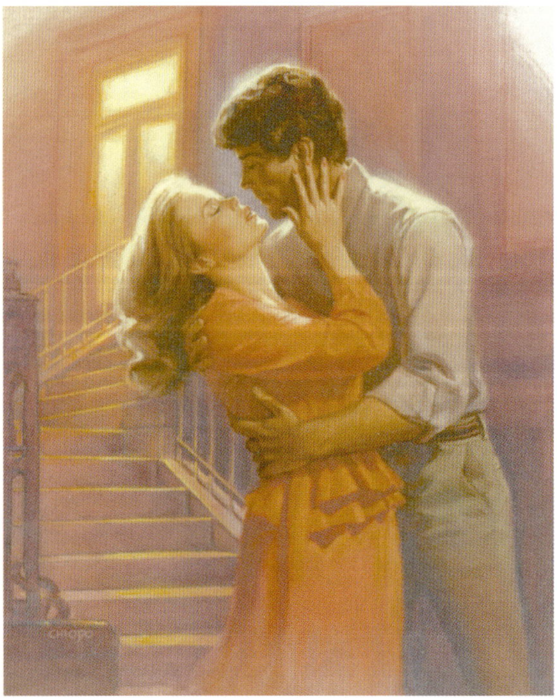

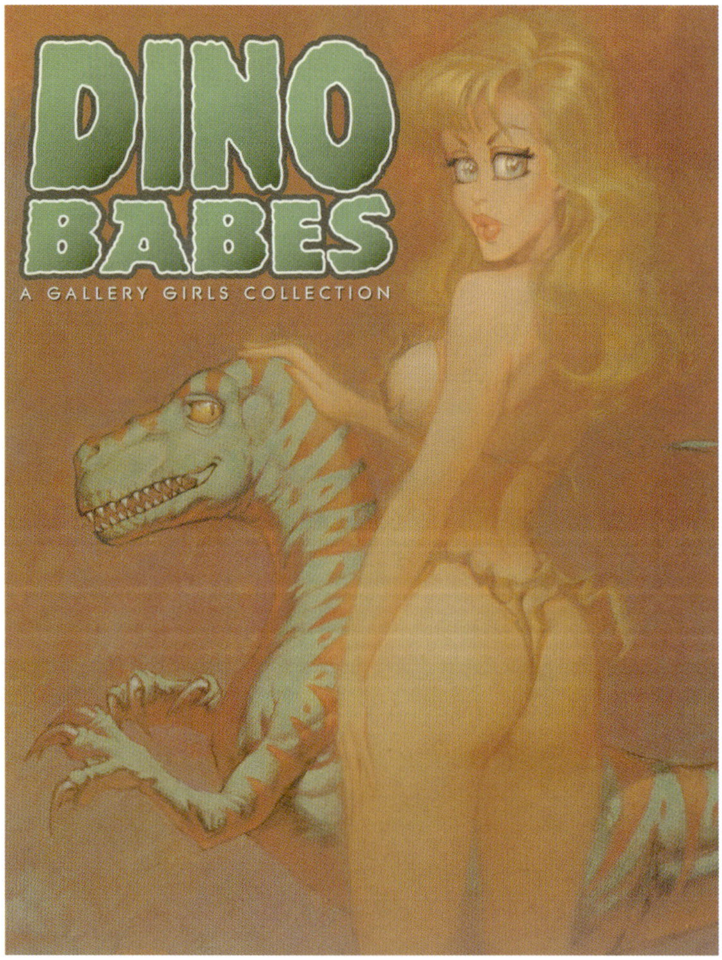

Left: Lovers, 1982, oil on board, paperback cover art, ©2003, the respective copyright holder. Right: Dino Babe, 1998, acrylic on board, *Dino Babes*, 1998, ©2003 Sal Q.

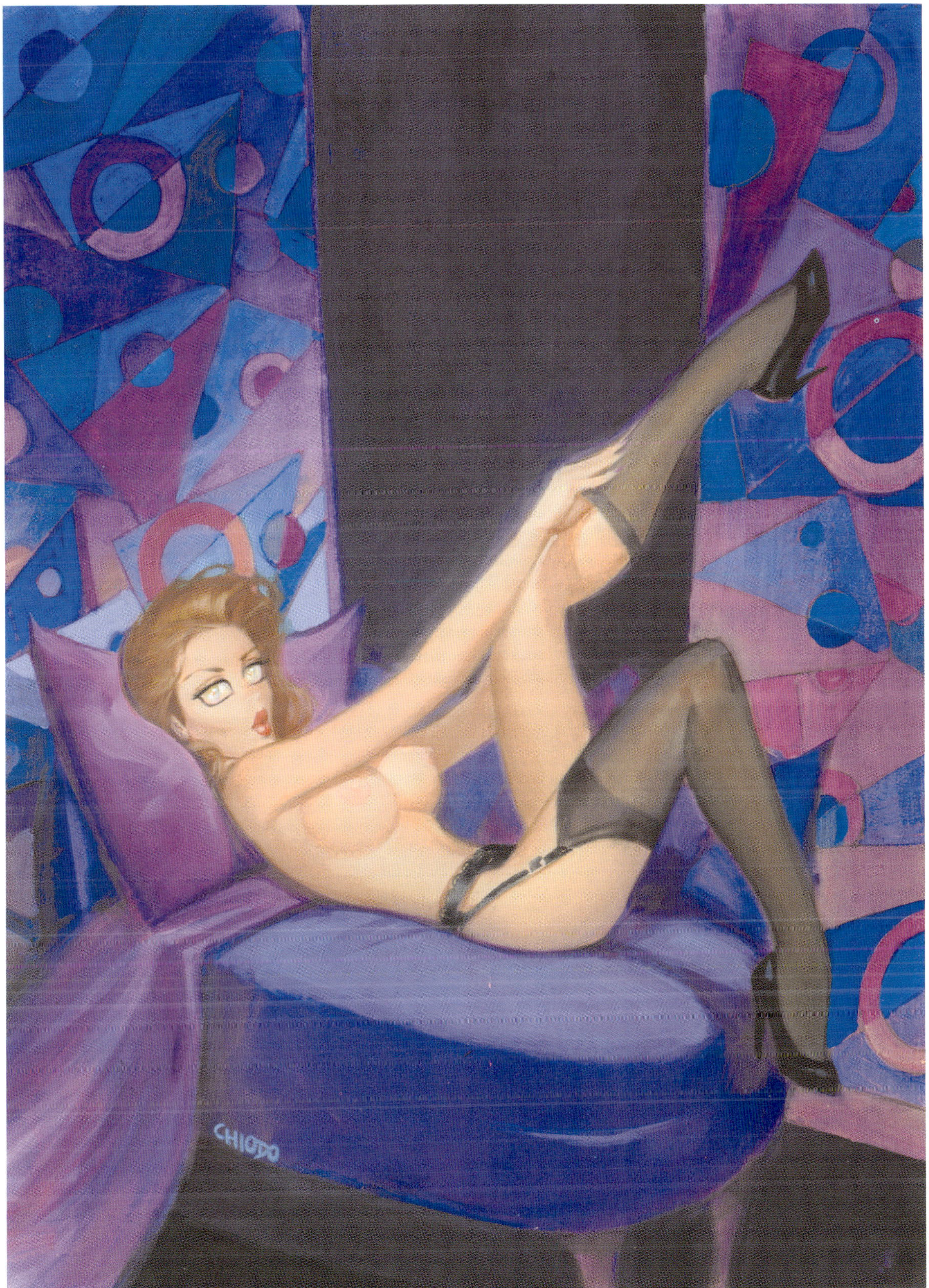

Black Stockings, 1998, acrylic on board

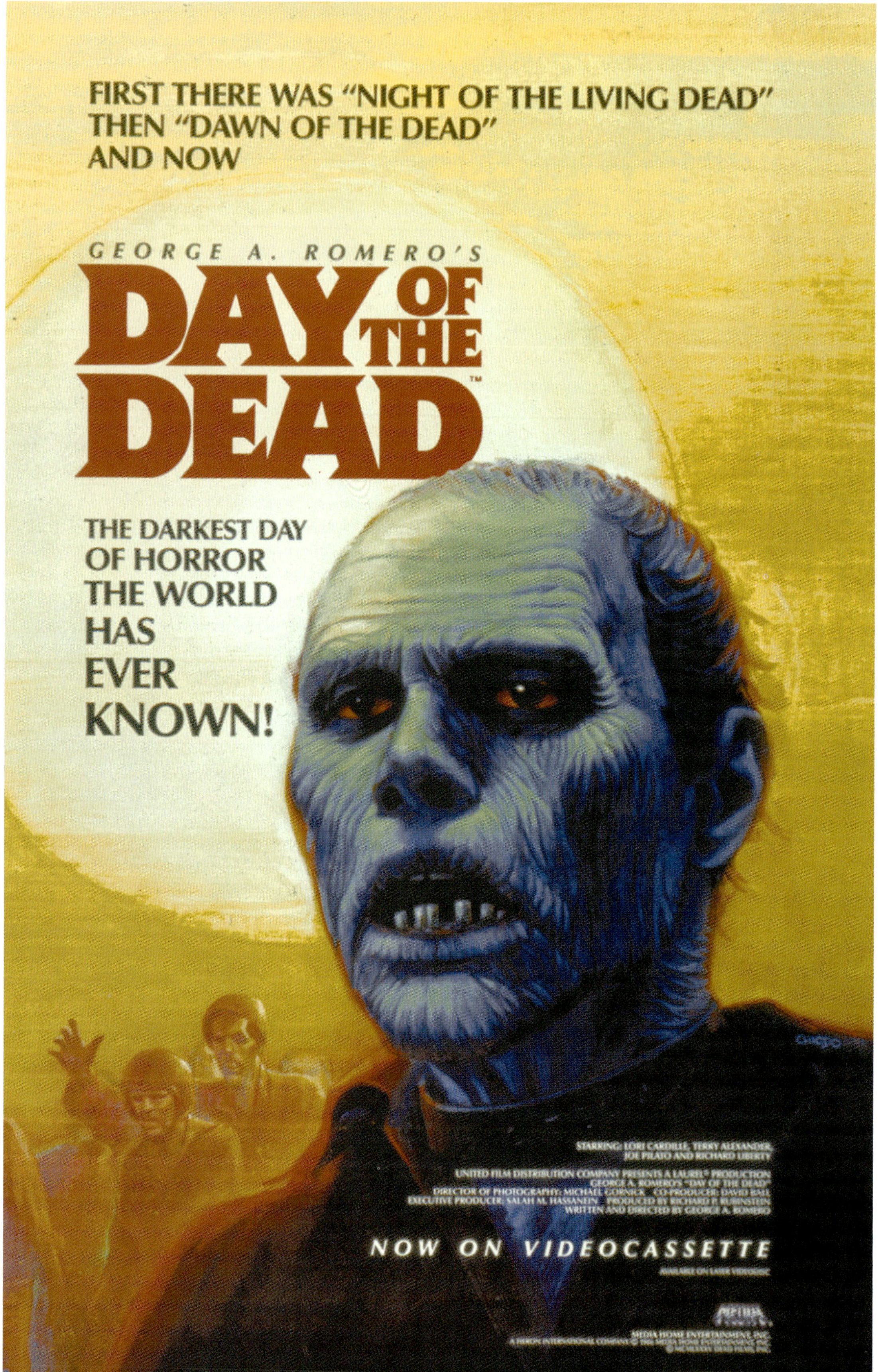

Day of the Dead, 1986, acrylic on board, ©2003 Heron International Company, Media Home Entertainment.

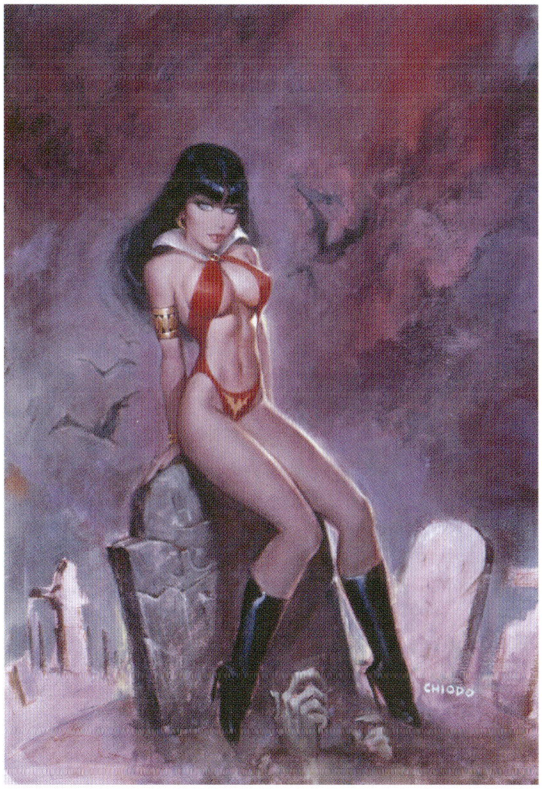

Gen13, *Pitt*, *Stormwatch*, *Wetworks*, and *Wildcats*. In 1993, he produced a fully painted sixty-four page graphic novel for Marvel, *Daredevil/Blackwidow Abattoir*, scripted by Jim Starlin. In 1996, Chiodo produced a fully painted set of trading cards presenting his versions of all the women from the Wildstorm comic book universe. Chiodo continued to work as a colorist and by the next year, 1997, he released the enormously popular book, *The Art of Chiodo*, a survey of his wide range of artwork up to that time. Chiodo was also hard at work developing his own graphic novel, *The Mechanic*, which was released as a forty-eight page fully painted book in 1998.

Recently, Chiodo has been hard at work on a number of comic book projects, and, of course, painting. "You never leave the comic book business," he observed, "but I am just focusing on painting for a while, I'm painting every day." Chiodo continues to paint "girl art" but he has returned to illustration and the work in this book is ample evidence that while he still has fun painting pin-ups, he is also revisiting figure painting, landscapes, and illustration. The chapters in this book give the reader a complete picture of Chiodo's twenty year plus journey into illustration, girl art, and comic art, and his most recent work is as strong, even stronger, than ever. Chiodo is also exploring the possibility of book illustration again, but for now he notes, "I'm happy painting and teaching, after all, that's what being an artist is all about." As far as working in comic books is concerned, Chiodo smiles, and says "I love comic books, and as long as books need covers, or they print comic books, I know I'll have something to do."

-DANIEL HERMAN

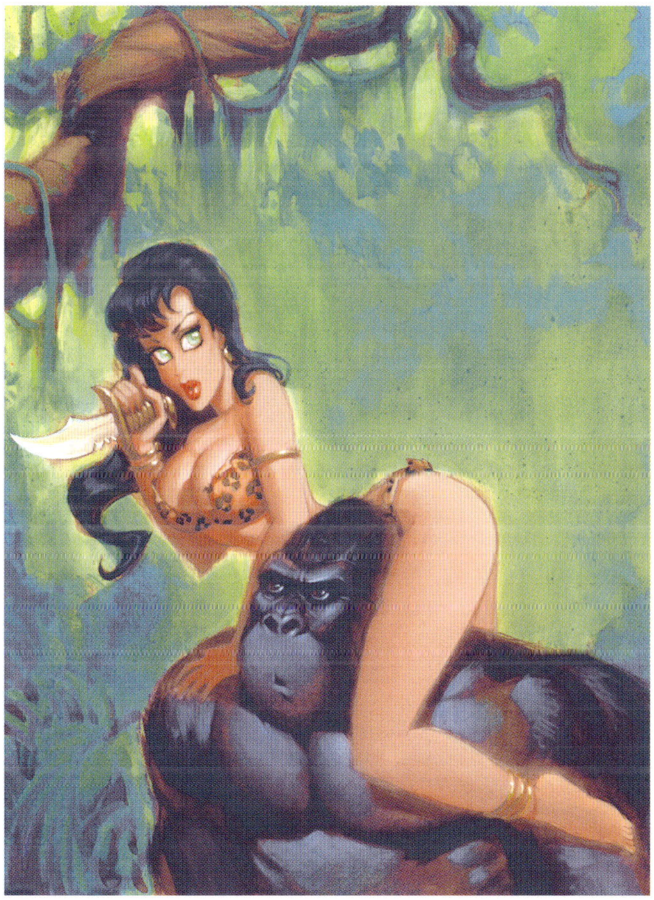

Above: Gravesite, Vampirella cover artwork, 2000, acrylic on board, ©2003, Harris Publications.
Below: Jungle Girl (detail), toy box cover artwork, 1998, acrylic on board.

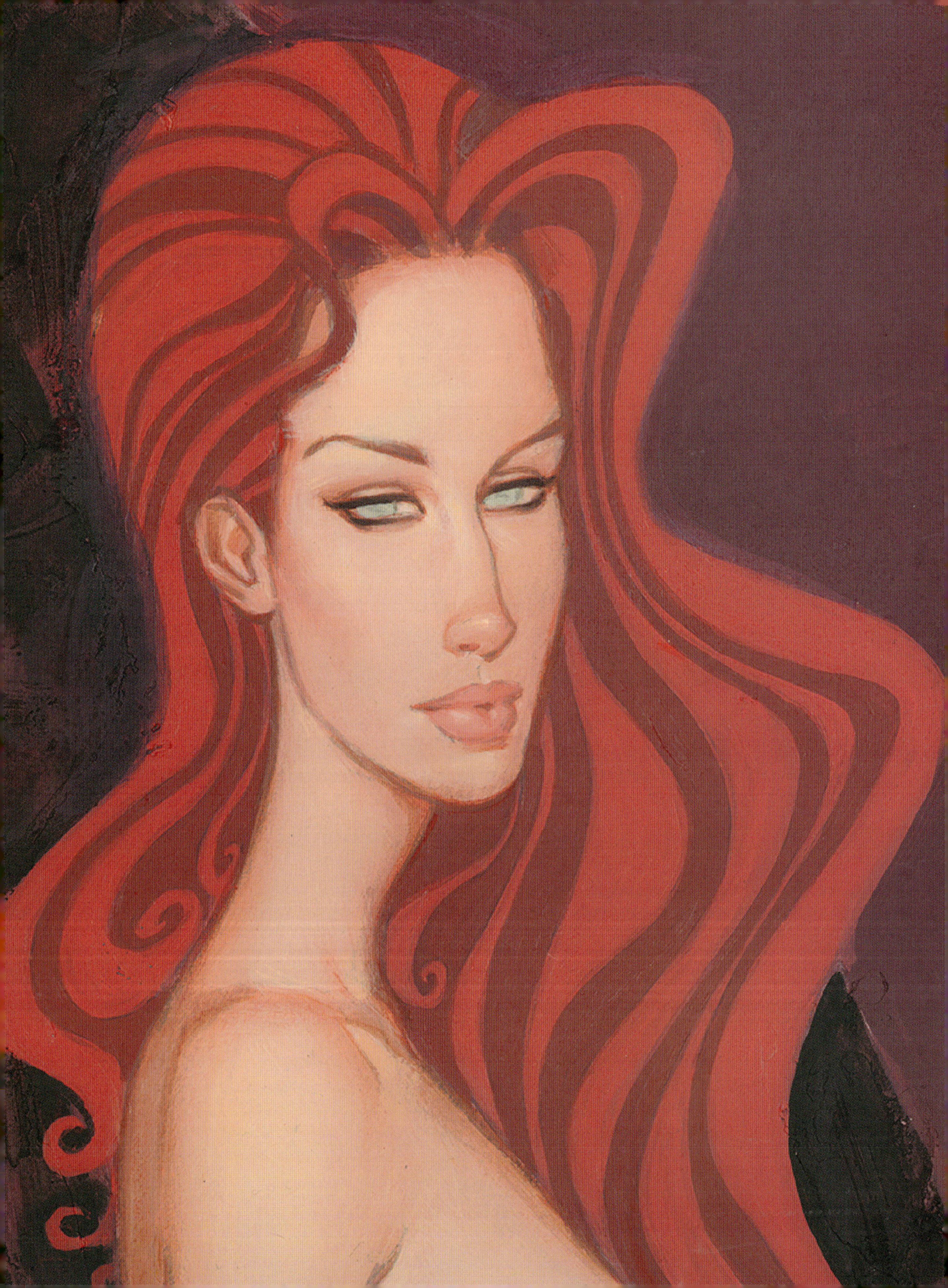

ONE

AN INTERVIEW WITH THE ARTIST

In preparation for this book, several interviews were conducted between Joe Chiodo and Daniel Herman. These interviews were condensed and edited for this book. The dialogue between Chiodo and Herman gives an interesting insight into Chiodo's past work in illustration and comic books and his current interests in painting and teaching.

DANIEL HERMAN: Unlike pen and ink work, which is most common in comics, which is conceptualized in black and white and many times colored in by a colorist with suggestions by the penciler, it looks to me as if your work is conceived in color and you have to be the one who is coloring it, because from beginning to end it is conceptualized as being in color.

JOE CHIODO: Well, I think that is true because painting and illustration are my background. I also worked many years during the 1990s as a colorist.

HERMAN: You started out in illustration and painting?

CHIODO: Correct, and as a painter coloring comics I brought that knowledge into the work I colored. Most of the comics I worked on were drawn in very linear styles, so I would approach them as I would any painting, by establishing form, cast shadows and separate foreground and background elements to give it depth. My approach is to consider all aspects of the composition.

HERMAN: What is your formal art background?

CHIODO: At a very young age I knew that I wanted to be an artist and I sought out other artists who were in that mind set and I just said, well I'm going to be an artist. I was always interested in art and I was fortunate to have a high school teacher, Rudi Franke, who opened my eyes to different forms of art. He would bring in examples of art from many different areas, comics, science fiction, the popular illustrators of the day, at that time I did not have favorites - - I liked them all. I especially liked artists and works that had more imagination than that of the photo realistic wave that was also happening at that time.

HERMAN: Who were the other artists you were associated with?

CHIODO: Well, I grew up in San Jose, California and although it was a big city, the small group of artists growing up there would gather together as we had the same goals of becoming artists. I was part of one of these small groups. A few of the artists in the group had made a trip to New York a few years before. Brent Anderson, another member of the group was planning a second trip to New York, so in 1979 we made the trip, we left San Jose for New York with not much more than our portfolios, suitcases, and sleeping bags. We made plans to

Red Waves (detail), 2003, acrylic and oil on board

stay with friends and just sleep on the floor until we could find an apartment. When you are young it all just seems like an adventure.

HERMAN: Well, when you went to New York in 1979, did you think you wanted to be an artist in comic books or did you just want to be an artist?

CHIODO: The interest for me to move into comic books came from a couple of directions, first it was all around me, I had traveled to New York with Brent, who was starting to make strides in comics. He had met several artists from a previous trip there and met more after starting work at Marvel. At that time all the artists would gather for regular social events, parties, holidays, volleyball in Central Park, and so on. Aside from the social aspects of getting into comics, it was the direction my book cover work was taking that made me take a look at comics as a way of expressing myself artistically. At that time many publishers had an account with a photographer and modeling agencies. You would get your script or synopsis, pick out your models and have a photo shoot. In some ways this was great as my work had a polished detailed look, but I found that it was not going in the direction I wanted, and far from the work of the artists I admired who used a more imaginative approach to their work. I still found that what I did was not that adaptable to comics, they did very few painted covers at that time, so I worked on some of the titles that were out there, *Savage Sword of Conan* was one, I also did a couple of short stories for that book.

HERMAN: Many of the artists who gave comic books a new look were in New York in the early 1980s. Were you interacting with other up-and-coming artists?

Oops, 1999, acrylic on board

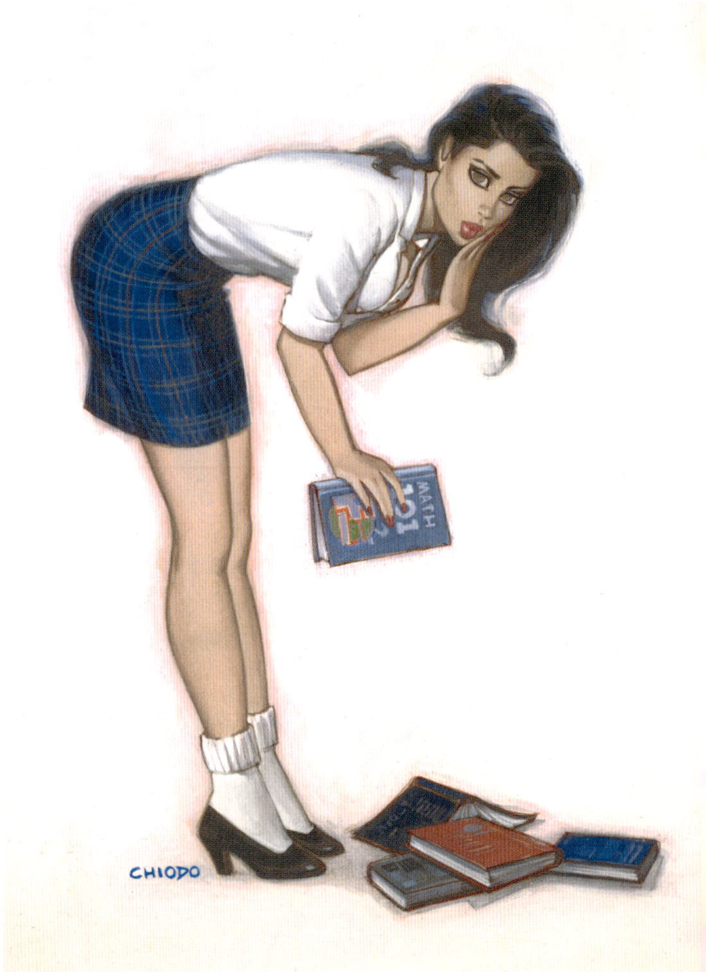

CHIODO: Brent and I were in New York for about two years when we met Bill Sienkiewicz. We talked about sharing a studio together. Bill was living in Connecticut at that time and his landlord had a vacancy so we moved into an apartment next to Bill and rented an office space for our studio about a mile away. It was not the ideal studio as it was in a small office complex, I remember the people in the office next to ours' complaining about our stereo being too loud. But it was a time of artistic growth for us. Terry Austin moved to the area and not long after Brett Blevins also came along and we had our own artists' colony.

Balance, 1990, acrylic on board

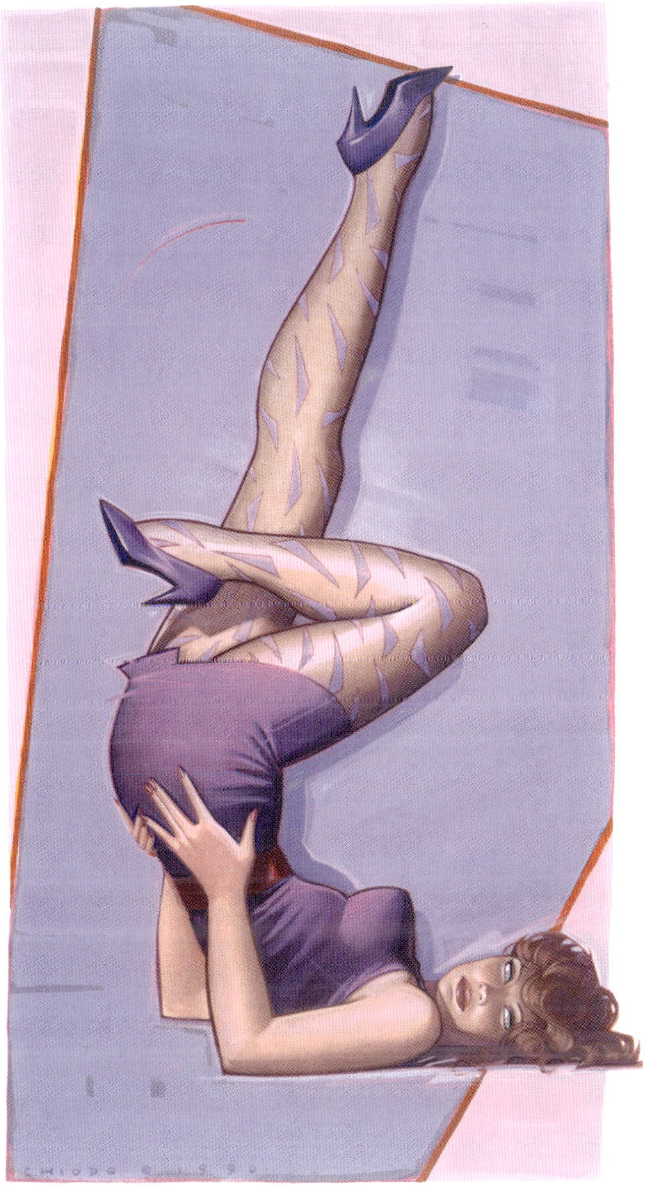

HERMAN: At this point in your career you were continuing to work in illustration, what were your objectives?

CHIODO: I continued to get book cover work. I always liked science fiction stuff but I always ended up getting into romance and western but it was a good experience though. It was weird because I was 21 and I was painting book covers! I did not care what the subject matter was at that time, I was so happy to get work I did everything that came along, westerns, romances, and science fiction. At that age I was just trying to basically try to paint and I wasn't really trying to do a specific style of illustration, I was just trying to find an identity.

HERMAN: I am intrigued about your setting up your pieces by going to a photographer and staging the scene and using it as a reference. I remember seeing pictures of Al Williamson playing Flash Gordon in photos which he later used in composing stories. To what extent were you allowed to stage a cover scene?

CHIODO: You could actually set up the lighting, put the models in and set up the scene the way I imagined it and in fact, I used Steve Holland, the actor James Bama used for his Doc Savage covers.

HERMAN: Everyone knows his face, Bama used him for a number of different covers in addition to Doc Savage. In fact, Holland was used by many other illustrators. You look at any number of book and magazine covers and there was his face!

CHIODO: Yeah, so here I am using Steve Holland as a model and I'm thinking this is great! The only problem was at that time Holland was so popular with artists you would go into a book store and he would be on a lot of the westerns. I had one art director tell me not to use him so often.

HERMAN. You were doing illustration and going in the direction of being an illustrator, why did you get in and then stay in comics?

CHIODO: Well, I was hanging around with

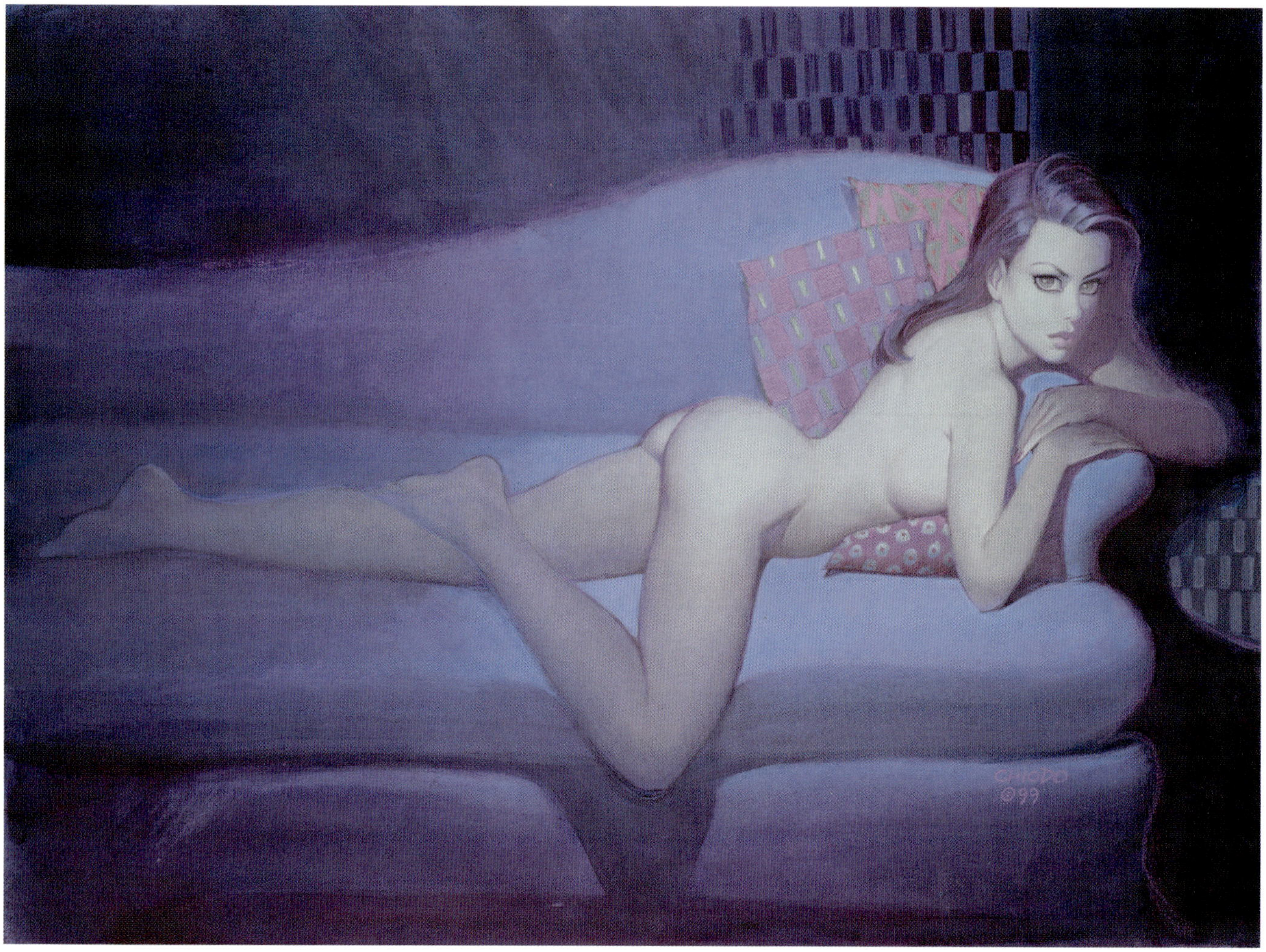

a lot of comic book artists and the more I looked at the potential of comic book artwork the more I became interested, so I started to say, well maybe I'll focus on the comics medium. I always liked the Conan stories, and sword and sorcery stuff, and as I began to appreciate the potential of comics, I became more and more involved.

HERMAN: You grew up in the 1960s, did that period have any effect on your artwork?

CHIODO: Yes, I thought the 1960s and 1970s were an interesting time to grow up. Culturally and visually there were so many things going on that, they are finding their way into my work more and more. I think because they did have such an impact on me growing up, I still do a lot of the fashions that were going on then such as the tie dye shirts.

HERMAN: You were born in 1958?

CHIODO: Correct.

HERMAN: So you grew up in the mid-1960s, were you reading comic books at that time?

CHIODO: I read very few comics, I remember *The Fantastic Four* was my first comic

Above: The Sofa, 1999, acrylic on board. Opposite page top: Cupid, 1997, acrylic on board. Bottom: Gotta Go, 1997, acrylic on board.

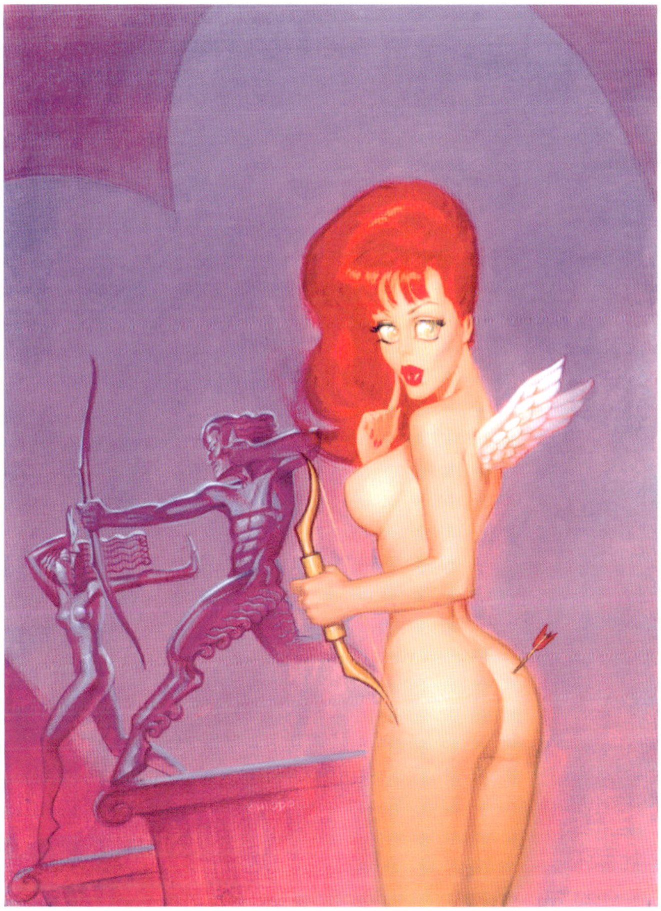

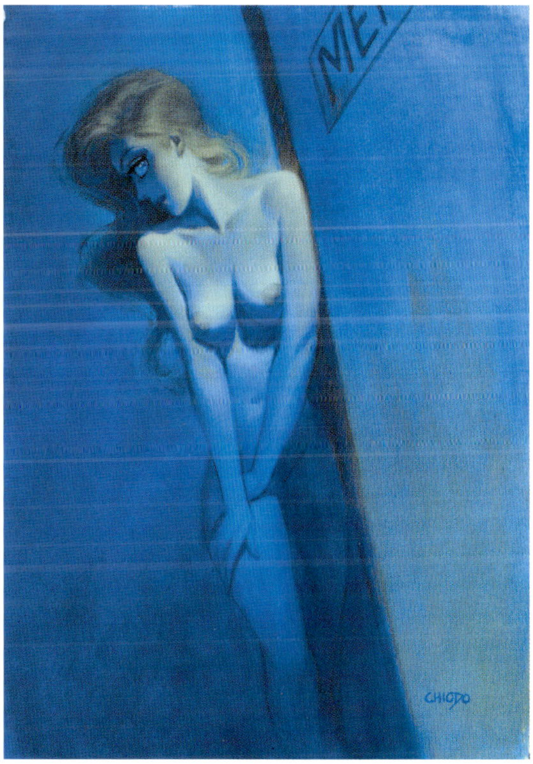

book and at that time, Jack Kirby was the artist. I remember reading one of his stories but it had no end, you had to get the next book the next month to continue with the installments. I ended up reading it and then the story was to be continued, and I waited an entire month, which was an eternity at that point, and I ended up not being really interested. It wasn't until the mid-1970s that I got into comics and I was more attracted to the stories in the Warren books, their format, where you would have a complete story.

HERMAN: You have a diverse range of commercial work, from comic books to paperback book covers and posters. Is there a difference in the mind set going from one type of commercial illustration to say comic books?

CHIODO: I think when you are doing illustrations you have to keep in mind what it's for and how big it will be printed. For example, most books are published fairly small so when I do a painting I will always work larger and when it is published at the smaller size it will look more detailed, but the mind set of working is always the same.

HERMAN: You are known in comic books for providing completely finished artwork, and color is a main ingredient in your work. Many of the artists going into comic books in the late 1970s and early 1980s tried to completely integrate painting and comic book storytelling. Do you see the artist as having more control over the final product as something that evolved during the 1980s?

CHIODO: Traditional comics spawned artists who had to evolve their talents and to use a team approach. They would do this

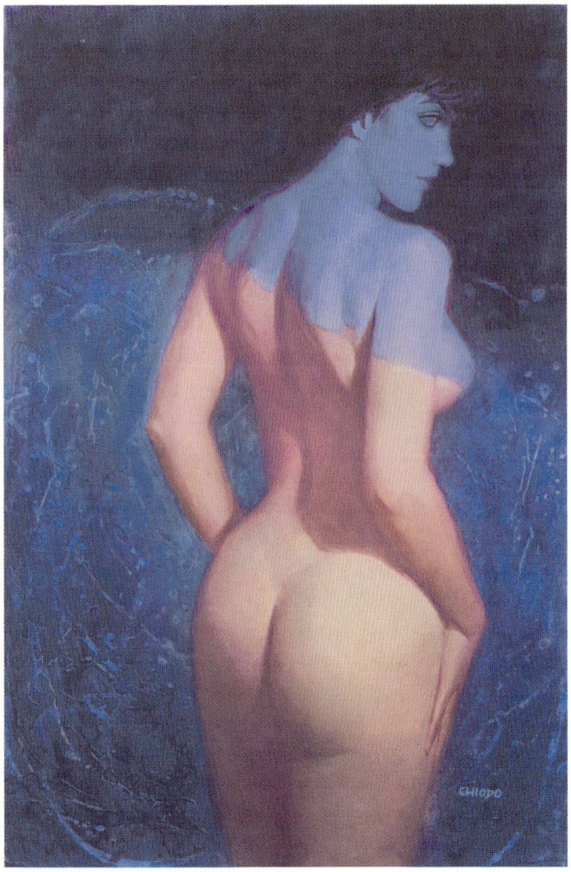

mainly to meet the difficult deadlines to produce a monthly comic. The team would usually consist of a writer, penciler, inker, letterer, colorist. I have worked on some of these teams over the years, mainly as a colorist. As far as working on the completely finished art, I have completed several projects, however, because completing all the art yourself they are all special projects with much longer deadlines than the regular comics.

HERMAN: Your work also emphasizes the feminine form. Your art in comic books seems to synthesize many of the aspects of pin-up art and comic book action and storytelling, was that your intention?

CHIODO: I think that whatever was evolving did so after doing several graphic novels, when you're doing these long projects you do work that takes all your efforts and interest. So by doing so much work you find things that work for you artistically, so you start adding to your repertoire.

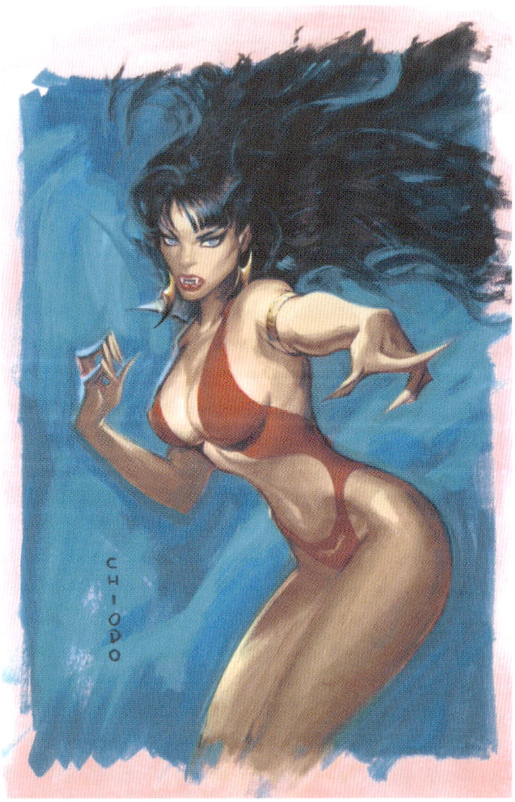

HERMAN: Much of the work in your new book was done in the last two years. The work is more painterly than your comic book work, what direction are you headed in?

CHIODO: The work in this book represents kind of a resurrection of my enthusiasm towards art. I had worked very hard for so long that I had burned out. It was like I was going through the motions getting the work done and having no connection to it. It was frustrating, I had to find a way to regain my enthusiasm. So I started taking art classes painting from life, it took a while and I started to progress artistically. The enthusiasm followed and the direction seems to

Top: Light and Shadow, 2000, oil on board. Bottom: The Evil, Vampirella trading card artwork, 1998, acrylic on board, ©2003 Harris Publications.

Unpublished cosmetic advertisement, 1989, acrylic on board

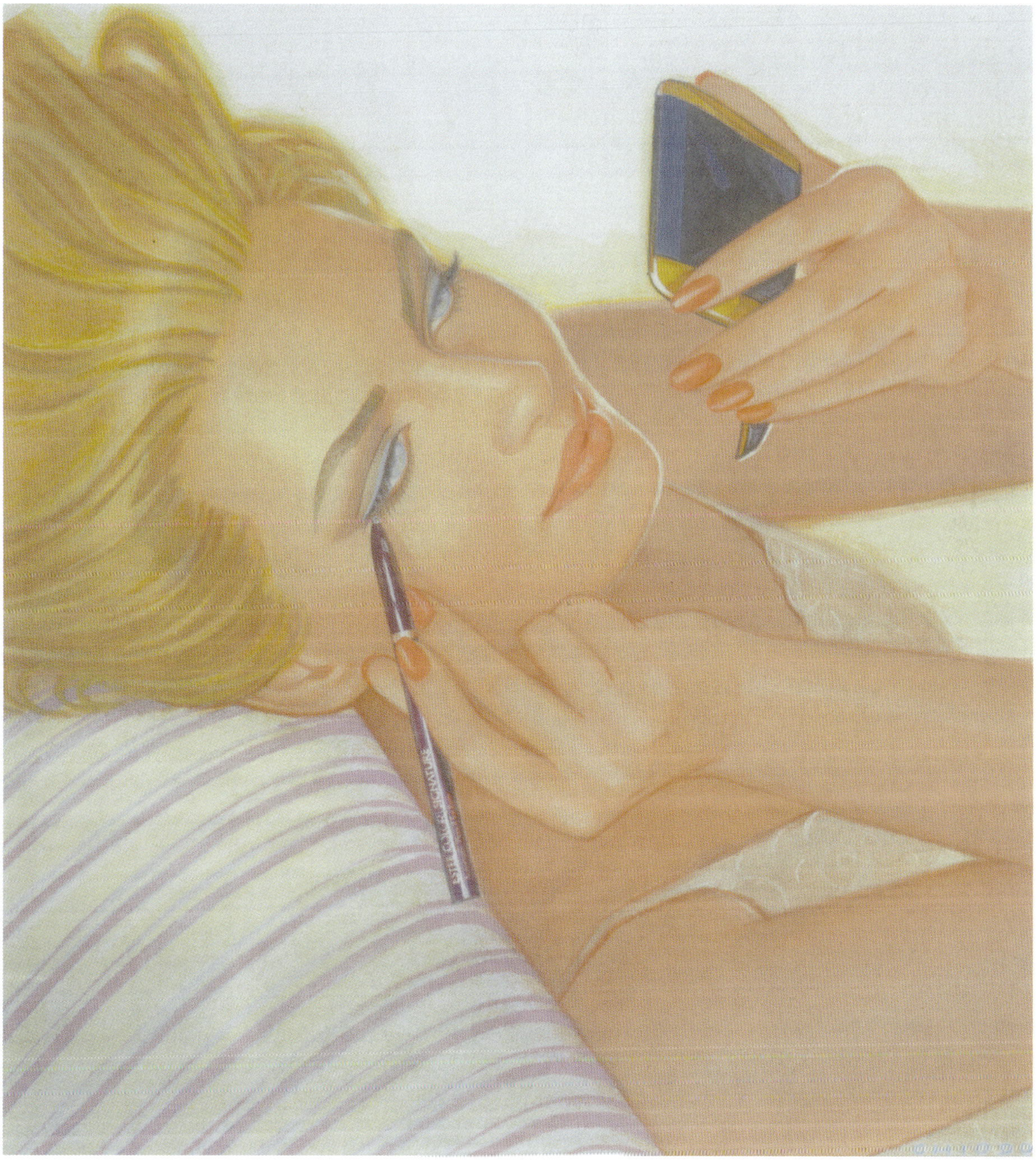

take the work to all the interests I have.

HERMAN: Your new work, however, does not abandon your emphasis on girl art, although in that vein you seem to be exploring new possibilities, for example, the lava light paintings, do you agree?

CHIODO: The current work seems to be going in several directions but to me they are all part of my development as an artist. There seems to be common elements that are consistent within the work, which would be the emphasis on the figure dominating the compositions. The more exaggerated figures are experiments that I had been thinking of doing for a long time, to me it's almost a stretched out stylized version of my more realistic work. I find they are a lot of fun to paint and I may do more of that in the future.

HERMAN: You are also teaching art, do you find this challenging and/or stimulating? Is teaching affecting your perspective on your own work - - or getting you to look in different directions?

CHIODO: I recently started teaching at Jeff Watt's Atelier of the Arts in Encinitas, California. I had been taking classes and studying with Jeff for the past three years, and he felt I was ready to contribute to the school. I'm finding teaching has helped my work on several levels. The first being procedural in your approach, when teaching, students want to know how to step by step start and finish a painting. By verbalizing this information you reaffirm it in your own work. In addition to this, the school has provided me with enthusiasm from the students and teachers there.

HERMAN: Looking back over the last twenty-four years, you have worked on a very diverse and interesting number of projects over the years, are there some areas you still want to tackle?

CHIODO: Well, I am always interested in exploring something new, my painting is taking me in different directions but I never lose sight of the fact that there are a lot more things I also want to do in comics. I really enjoy working on my own ideas, and there are plenty more to come.

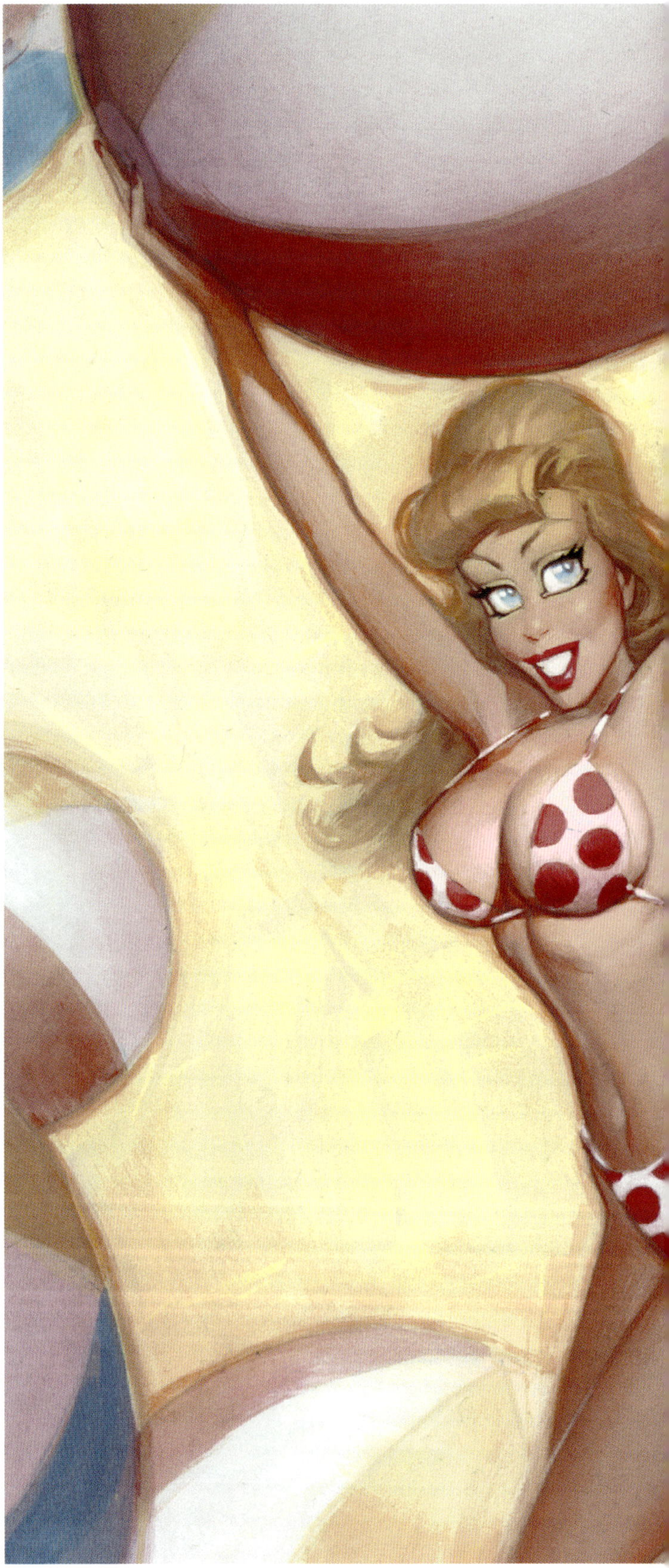

Bikini Babe, toy box cover artwork, 1998, acrylic on board

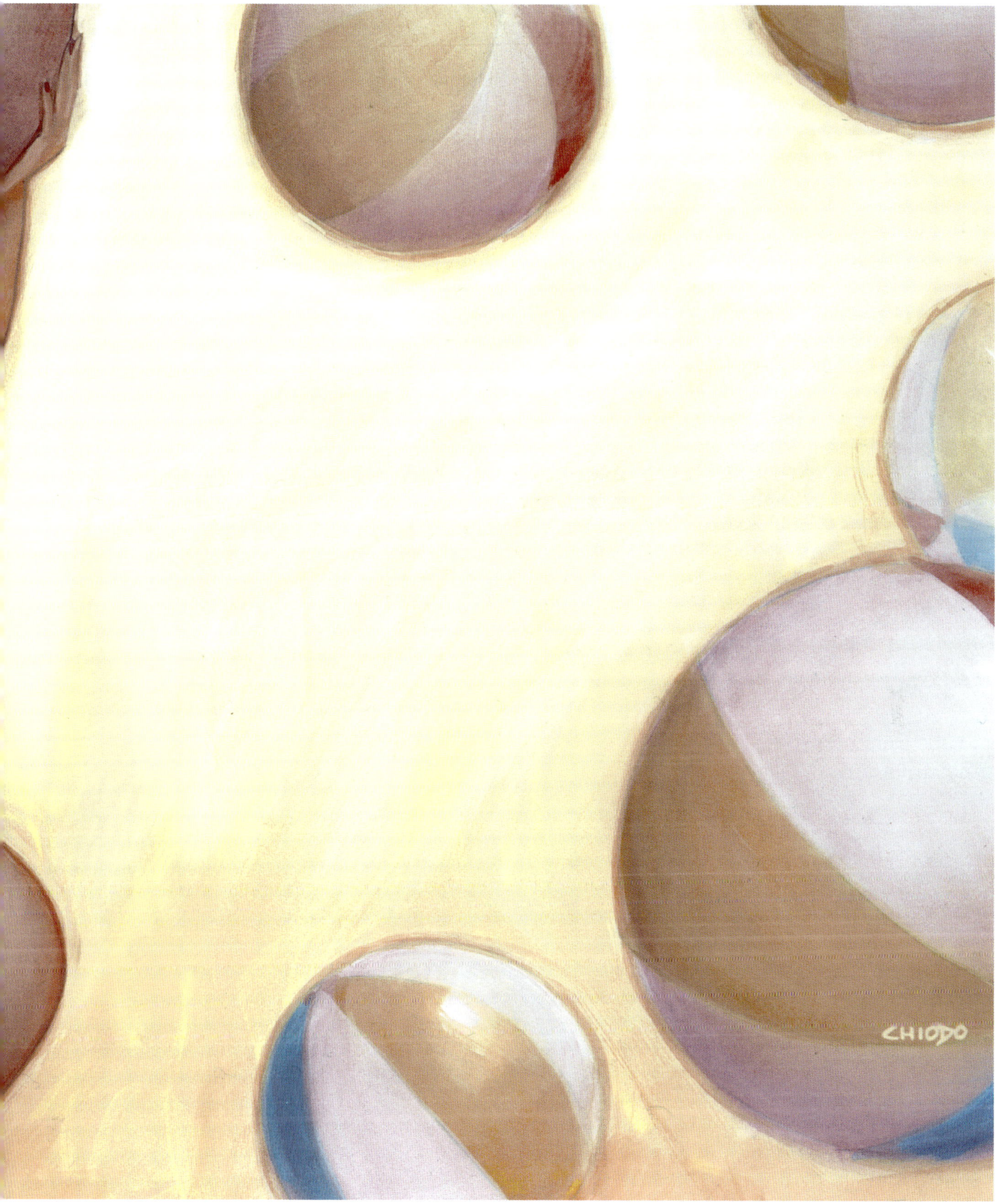
CHIODO

TWO
GIRL ART

The paintings on display in this chapter have all been produced in the last two years. This section is an exhibition, in print, of the diversity of Chiodo's work. Although all these paintings are "girl art," they showcase a breadth of style, color, and design which is genuinely exciting to look at. For those just looking at the women in these paintings, they are, as the old rhyme goes, "naughty and nice."

While all of the compositions in this chapter are great fun to look at, all the artwork in the section clearly fits within the great American art form known as the pin-up. The pin-up has a long tradition in popular American art going back to the "roaring twenties." Indeed, certain aspects of the 1920s, jazz, flappers, and the open sexuality of the time, found their way into illustration and periodicals of the day. Two illustrators from this period, John Held, Jr., and Russell Patterson are now fondly remembered for their depictions of the style and attitude associated with the 1920s. Held and Patterson had their work popularized by the magazines of the time and their women entered the lexicon of popular images of the era. Glamorous artwork of a more sexual nature was also being used on the front covers of pulp magazines as well as in calendar artwork by the 1920s. Although most of the work seen in the pulps and in calendar artwork was of low quality, more able illustrators were, nevertheless, also attracted to make their own contributions which demonstrated that talented artists can produce admirable work in any medium. The Great Depression saw a significant increase in the popularity of the pin-up, along with a number of distinguished illustrators contributing artwork for calendar and magazine illustration. The 1930s saw *Esquire* magazine featuring the work of George Petty (known for his "Petty Girl") and Antonio Vargas, both who became household names as a result of their pin-up art. The World War II era witnessed even a greater proliferation of pin-up art, which by that time was seen in magazines, on billboards, on fighter airplanes, ships, and in every soldier's mess hall. Since then, pin-up art has become a mainstay of American illustration. Chiodo's work fits securely within the history of the American pin-up.

The paintings in this chapter run the gamut from cartoon pin-ups to pin-ups with an art deco flavor. There is something for everybody, so enjoy!

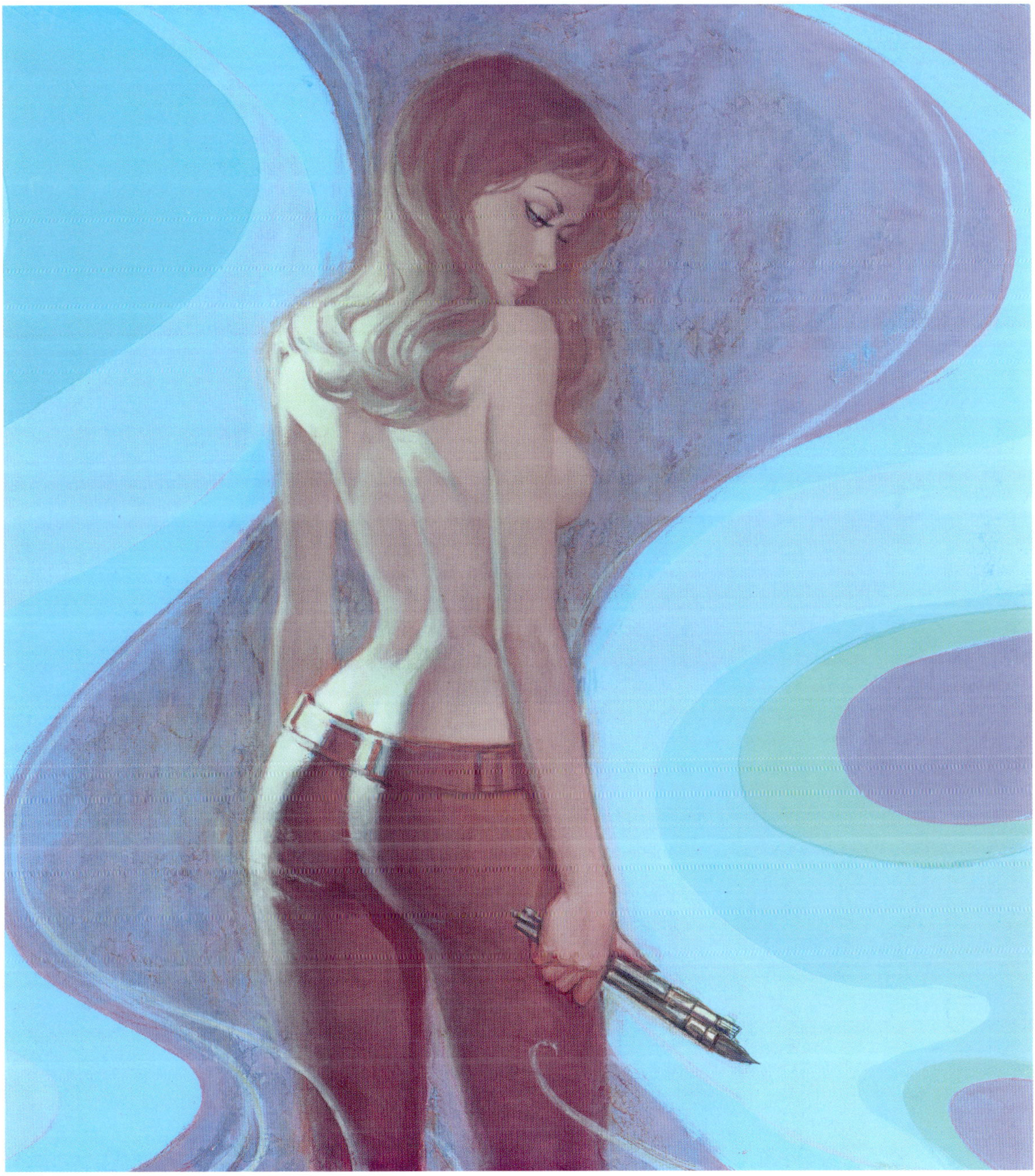

Painted Swirls in Blue and Green, 2003, acrylic and oil on board

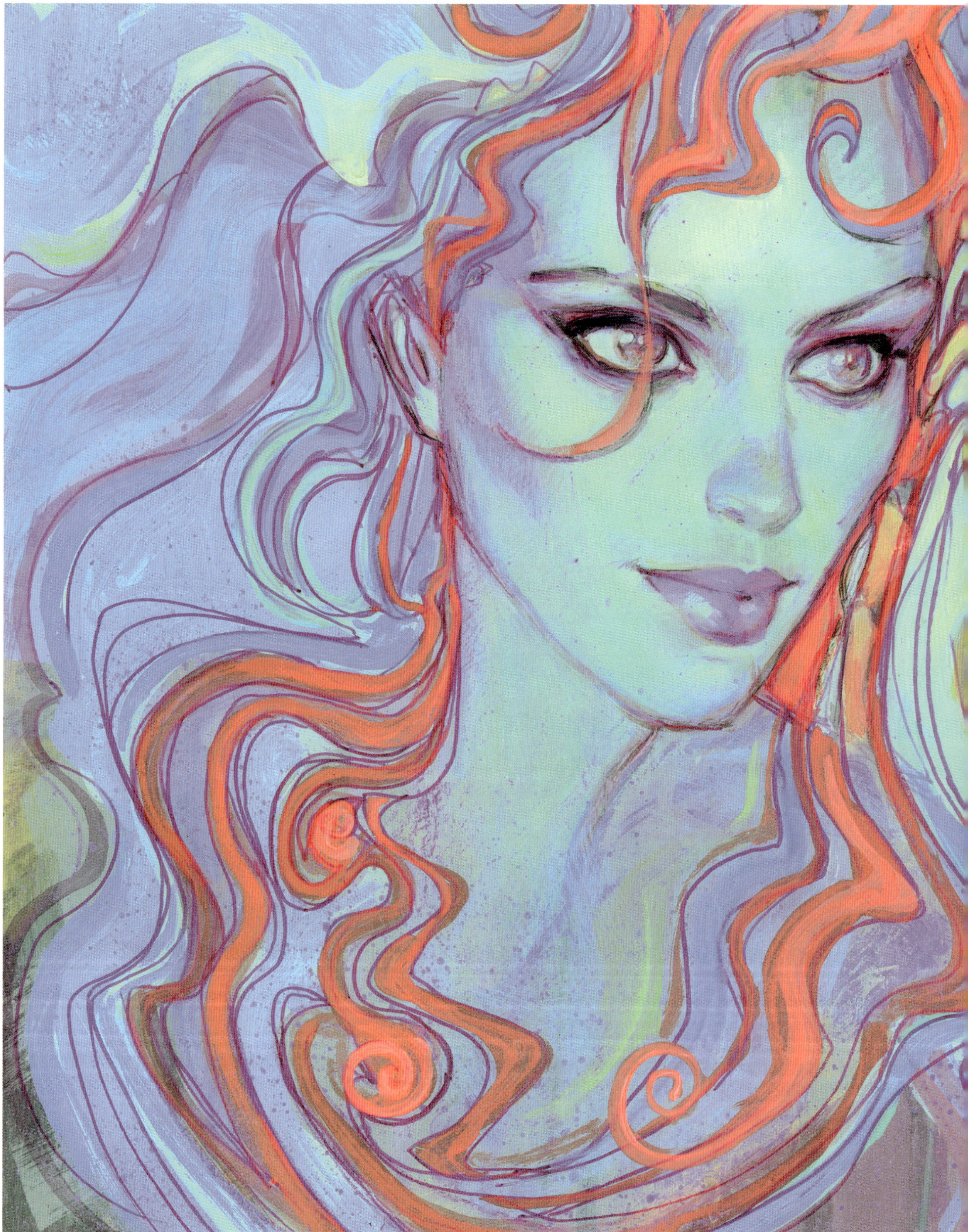

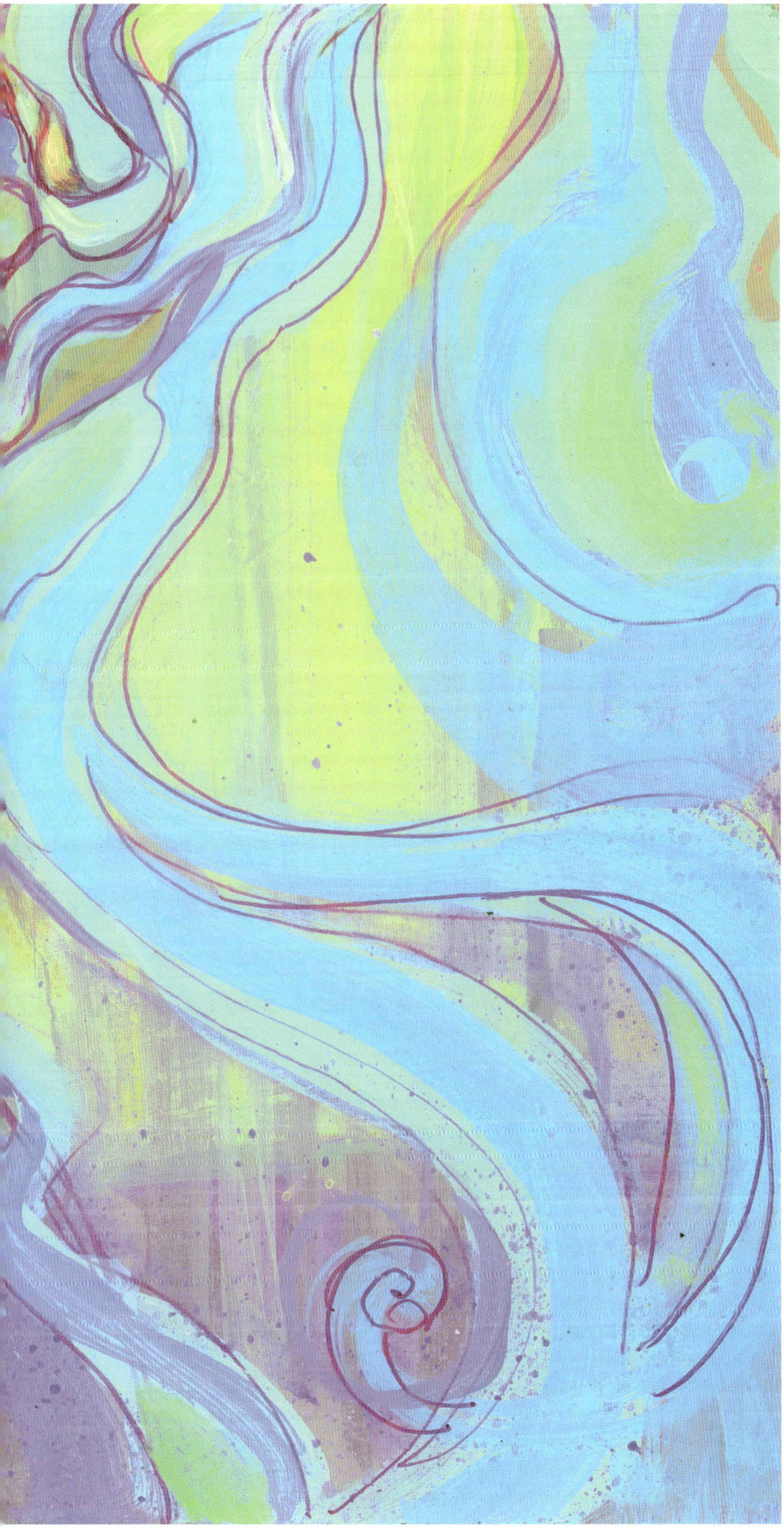

Free Form, 2002, acrylic on board

Minion, Vampirella cover, 2002, oil on board, ©2003 Harris Publications. Opposite page: Big Bad, 2002 acrylic on board.

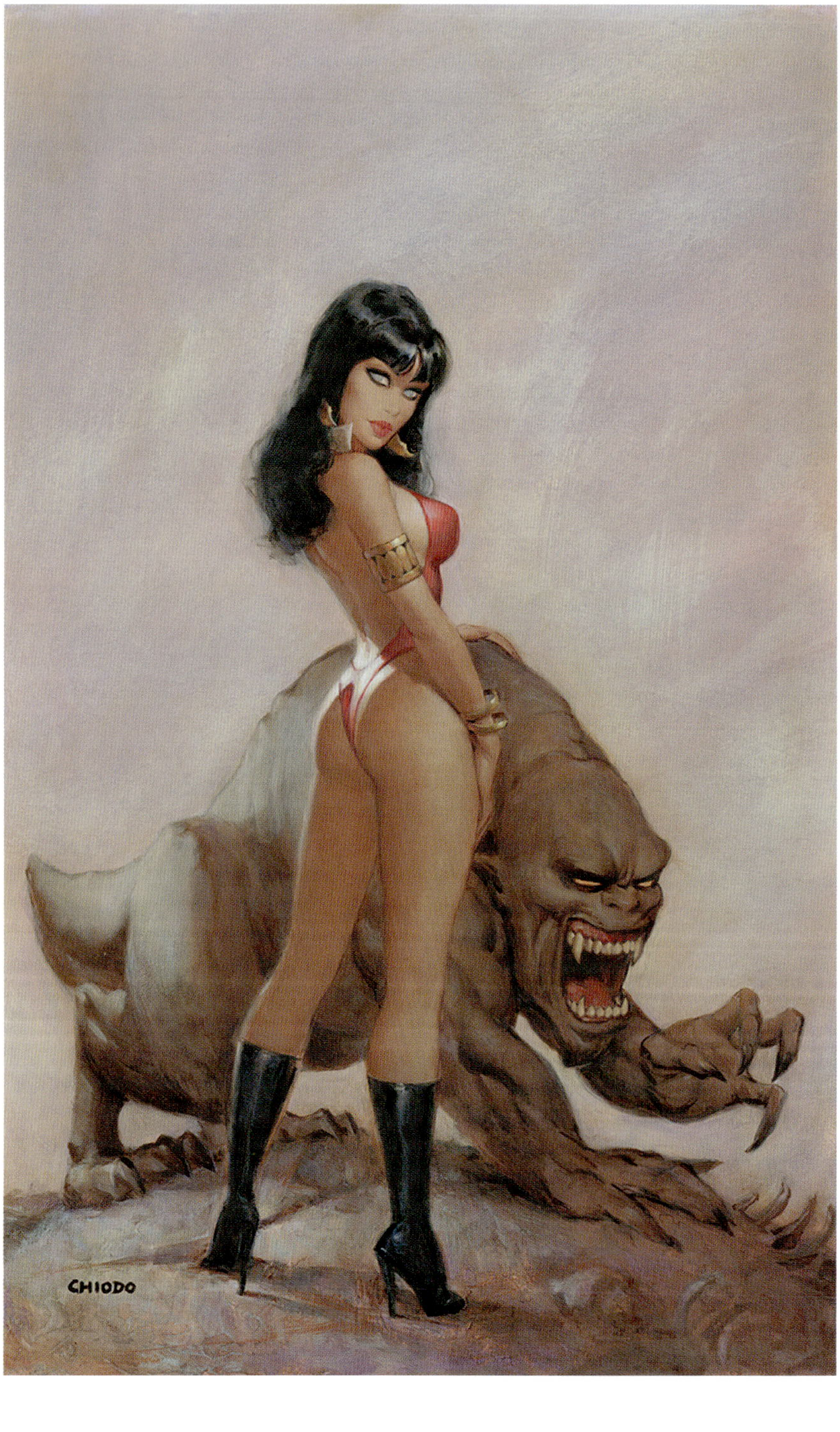

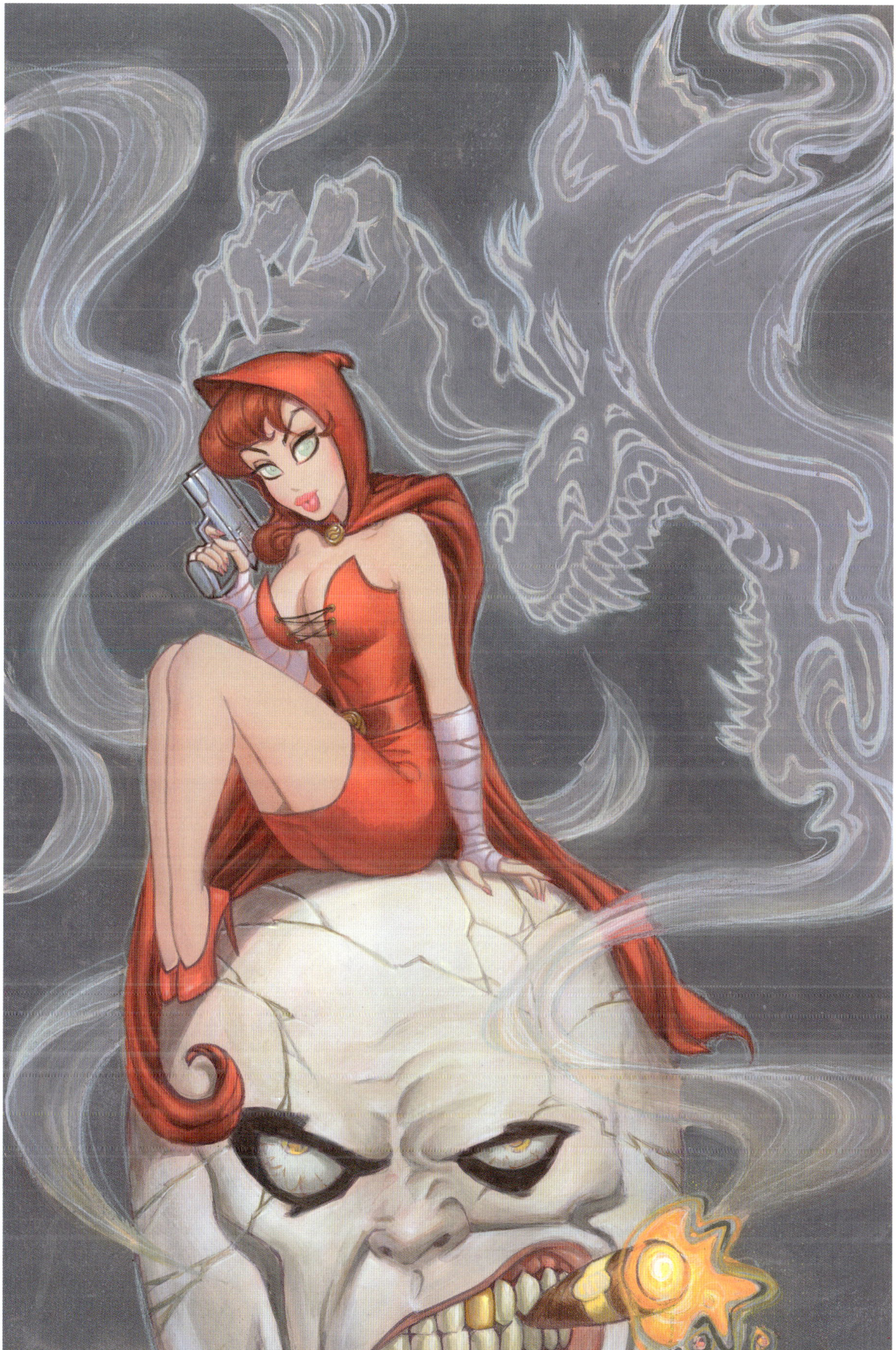
CHIODO

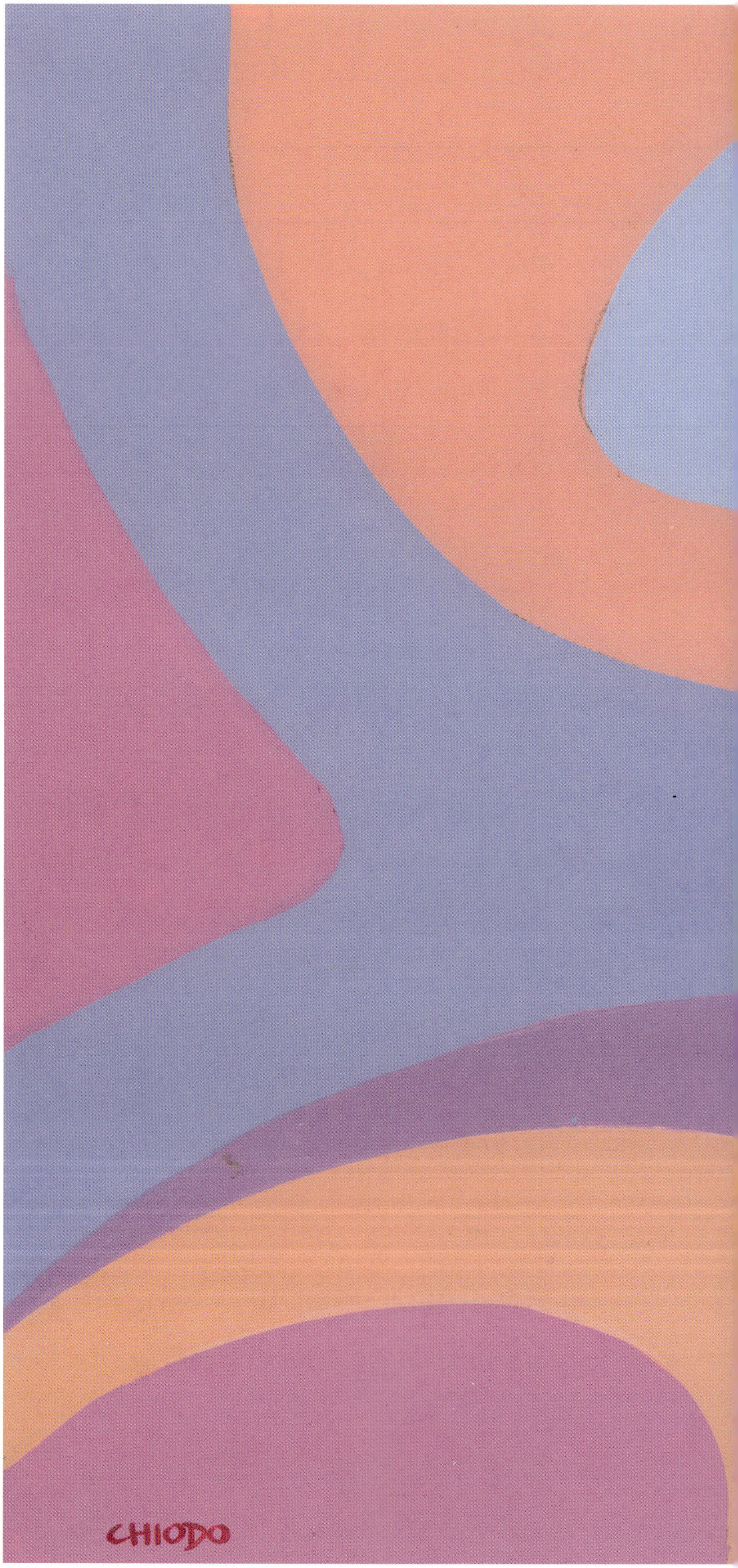

Color Clouding My Thoughts, 2002, acrylic and oil on board

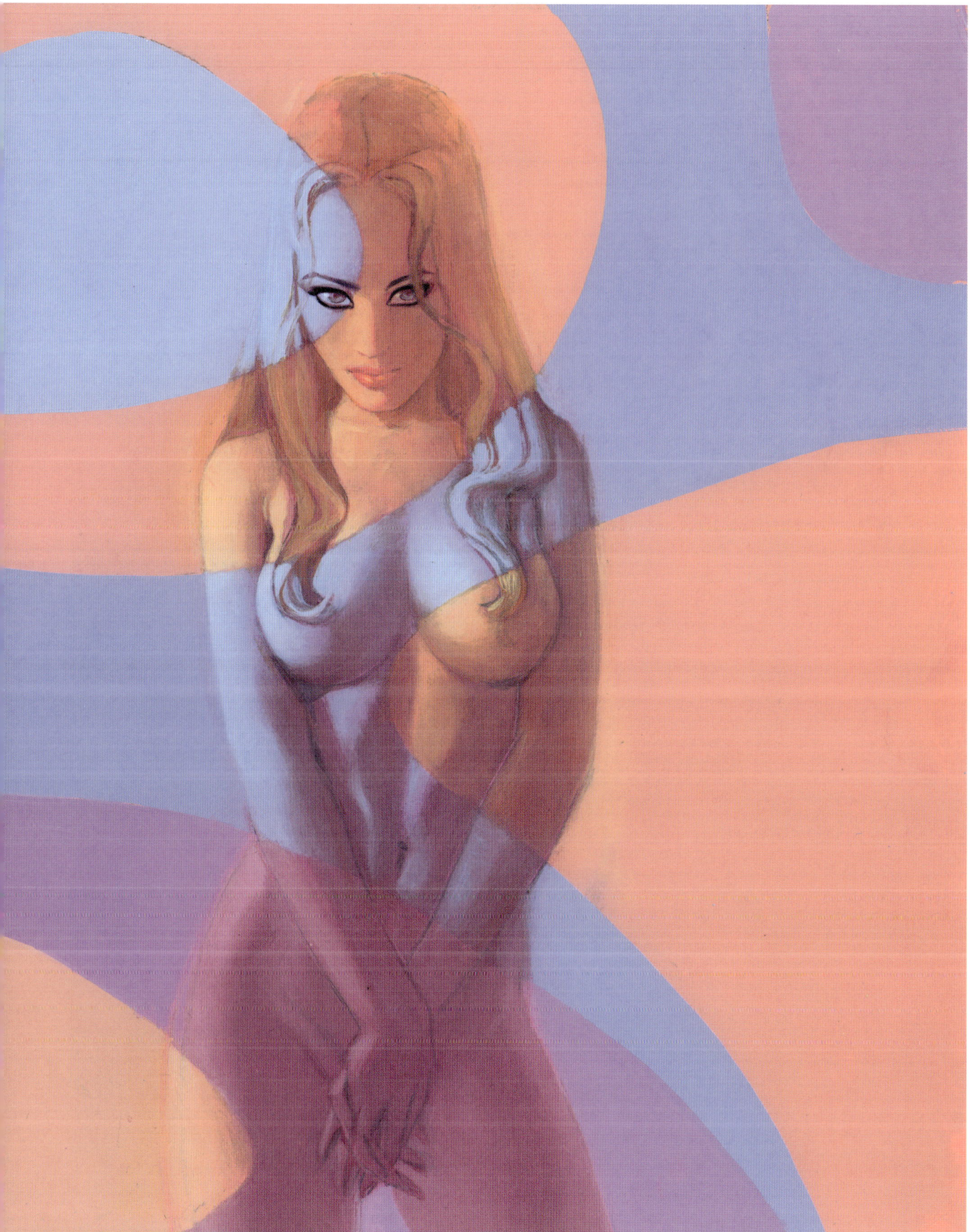

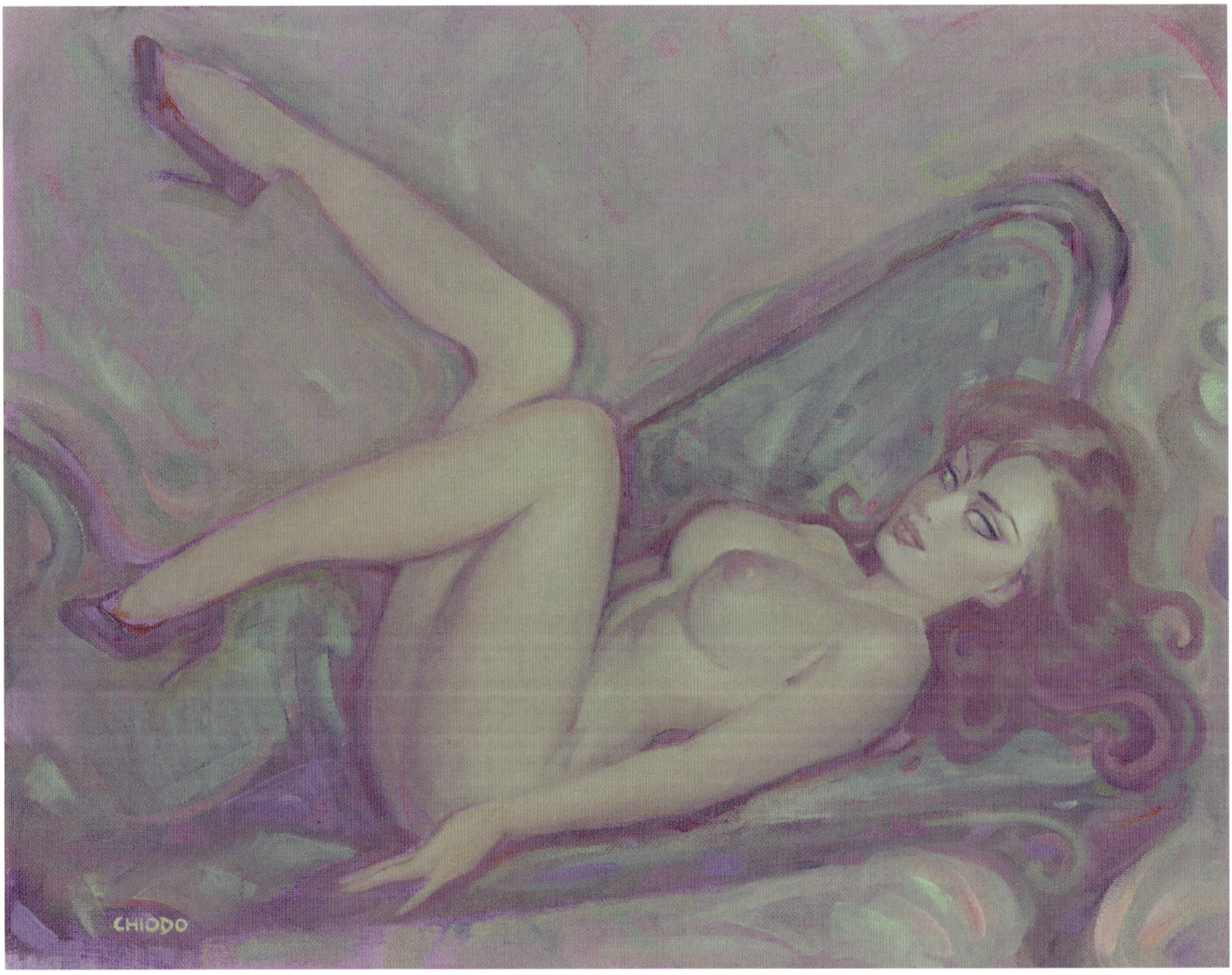

Heels, 2002, oil on canvas

Barb, 2002, oil on canvas

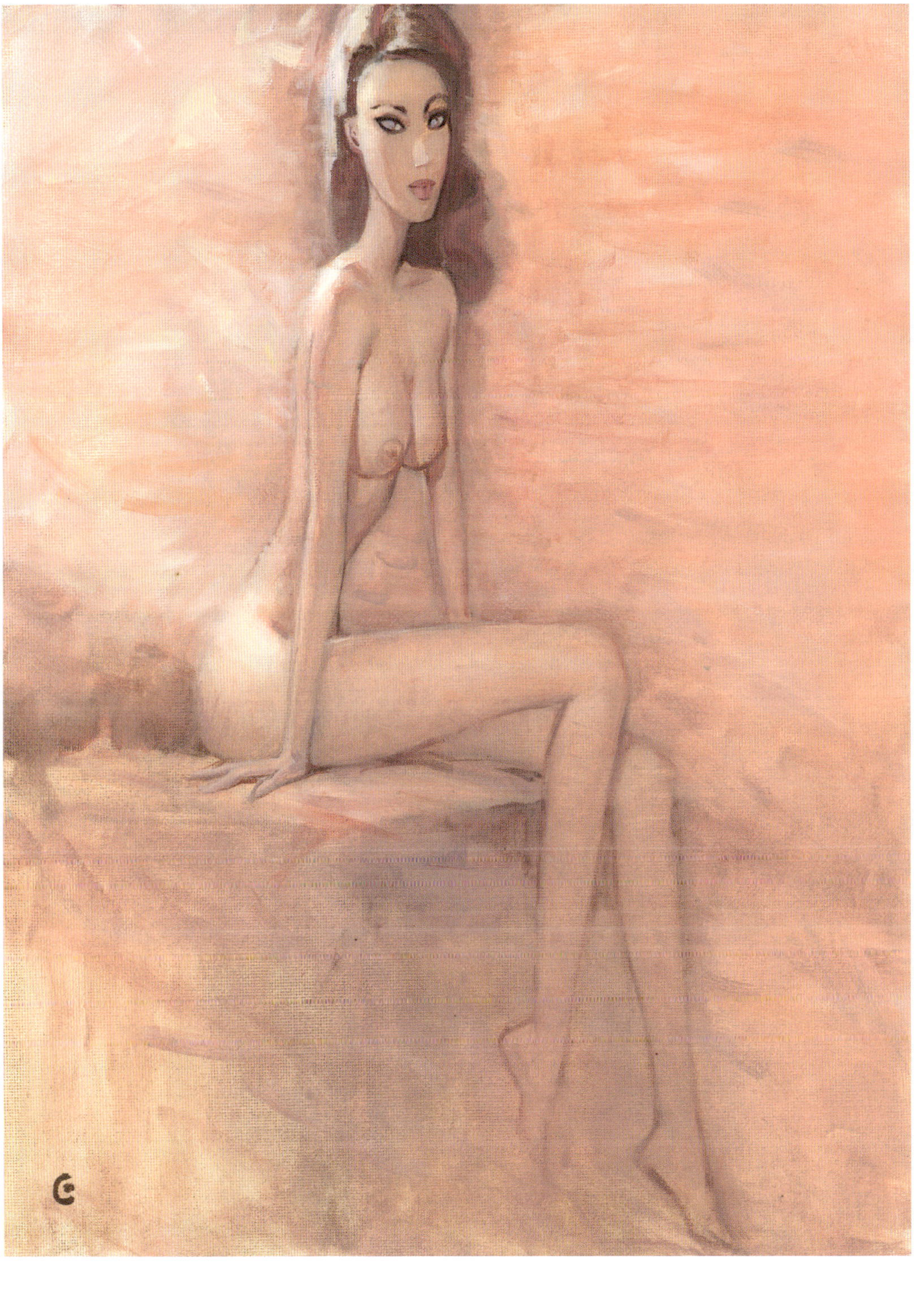

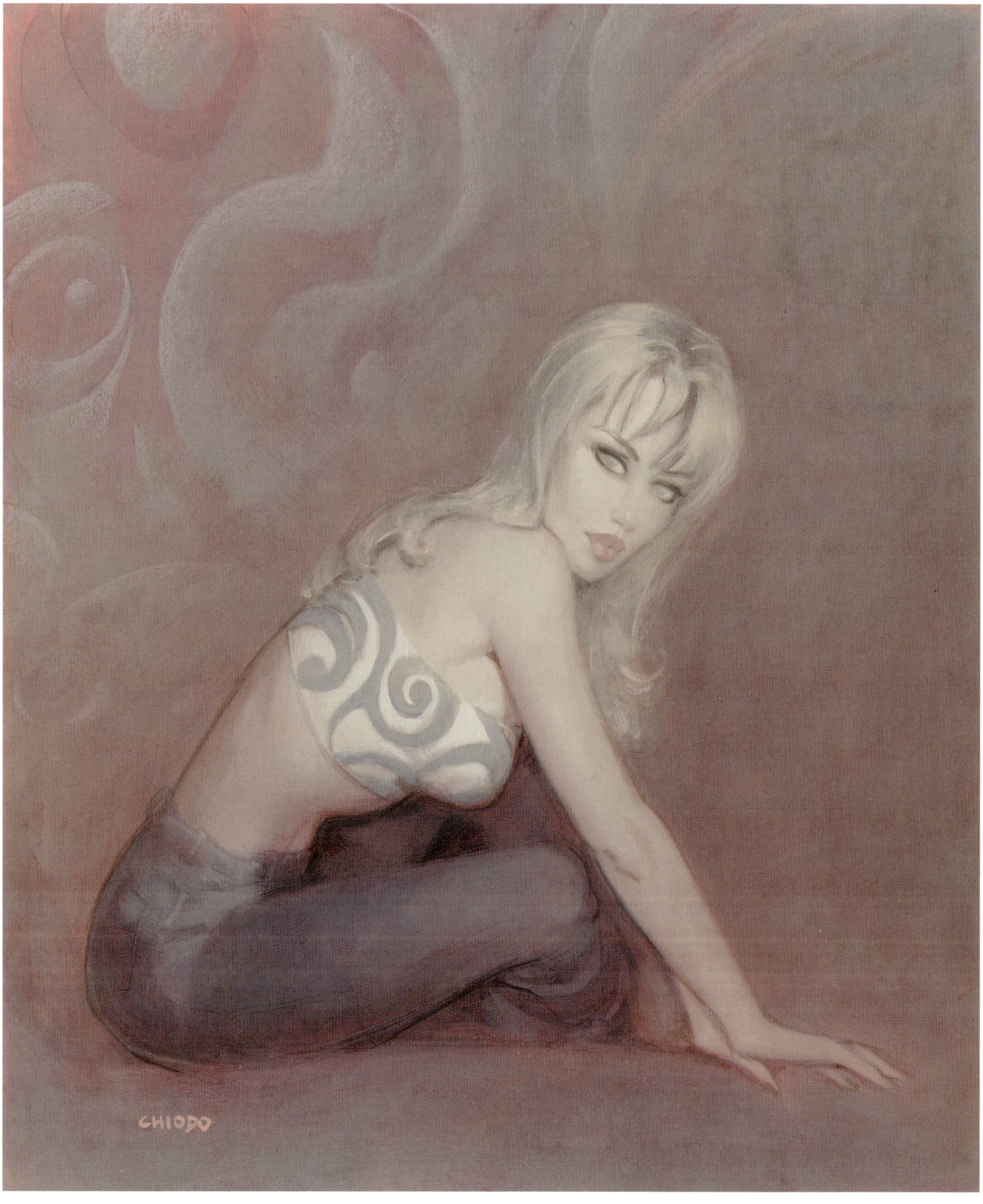

Crossed Legged, 2002, acrylic on board

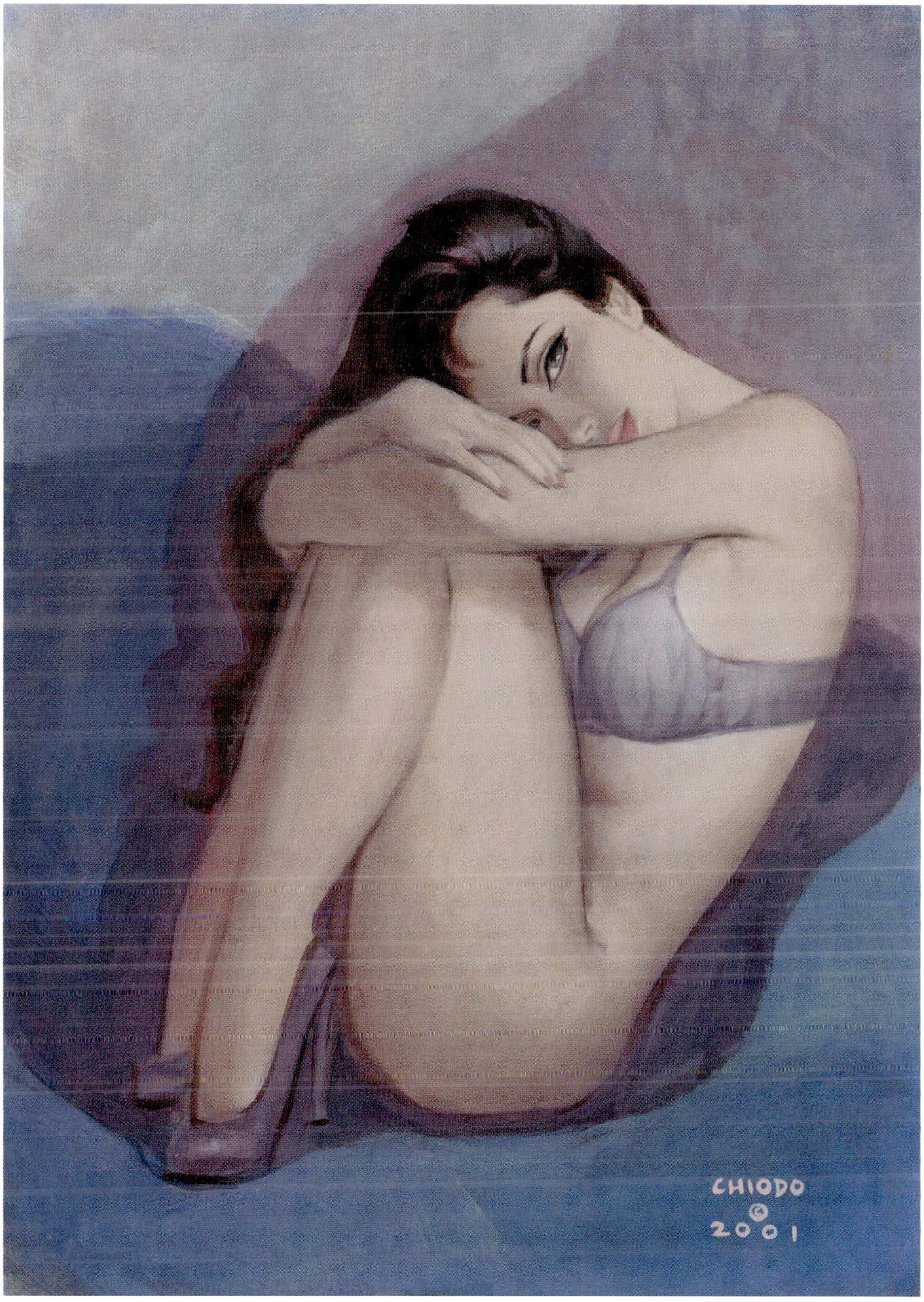

Sitting with Thoughts, 2001, acrylic on board

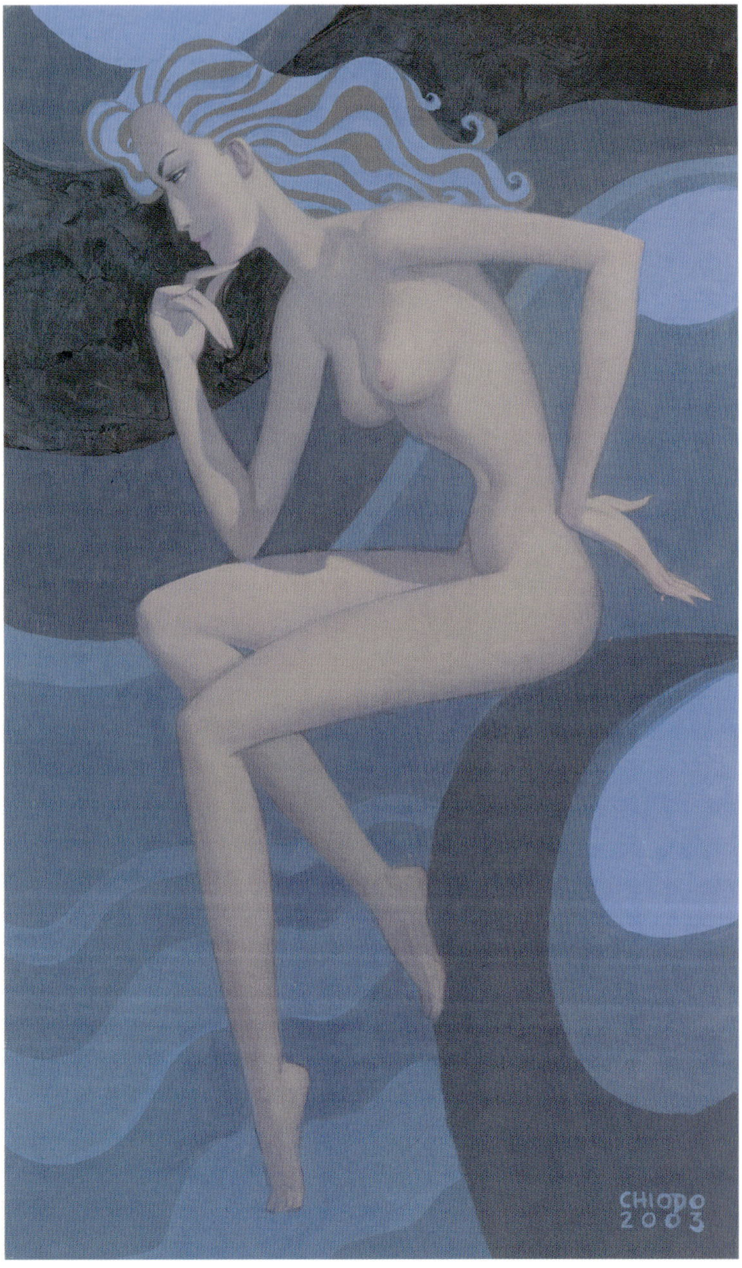

Thinking Cool Thoughts, 2003, acrylic on board

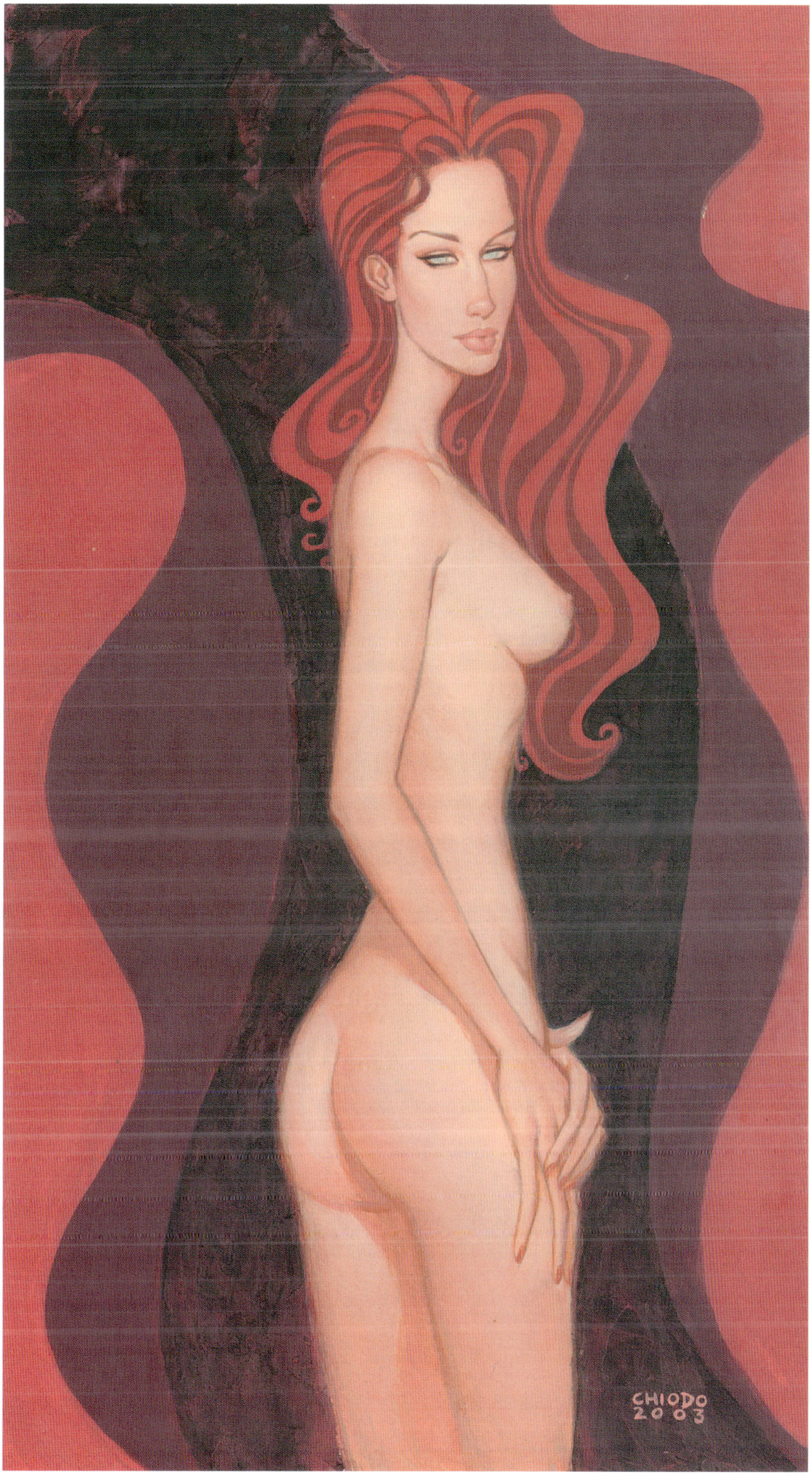

Red Waves, 2003, acrylic on board

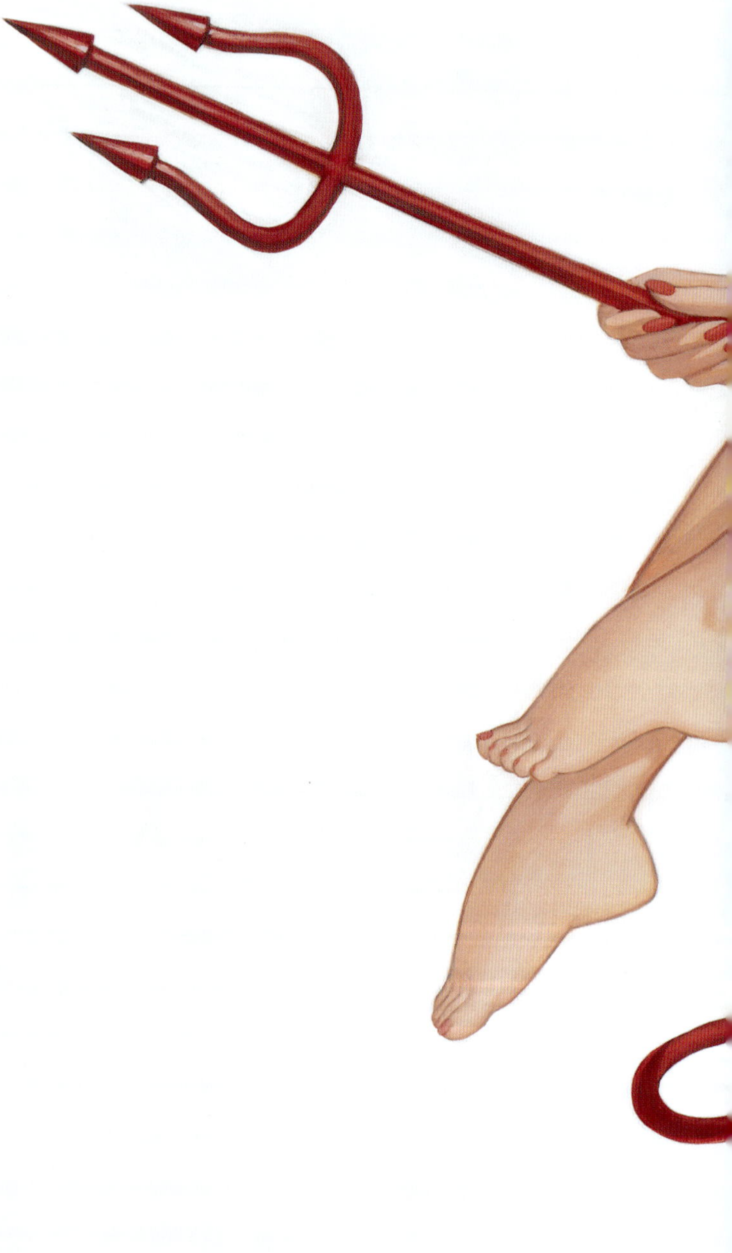

Red Devil, 2002, acrylic on board

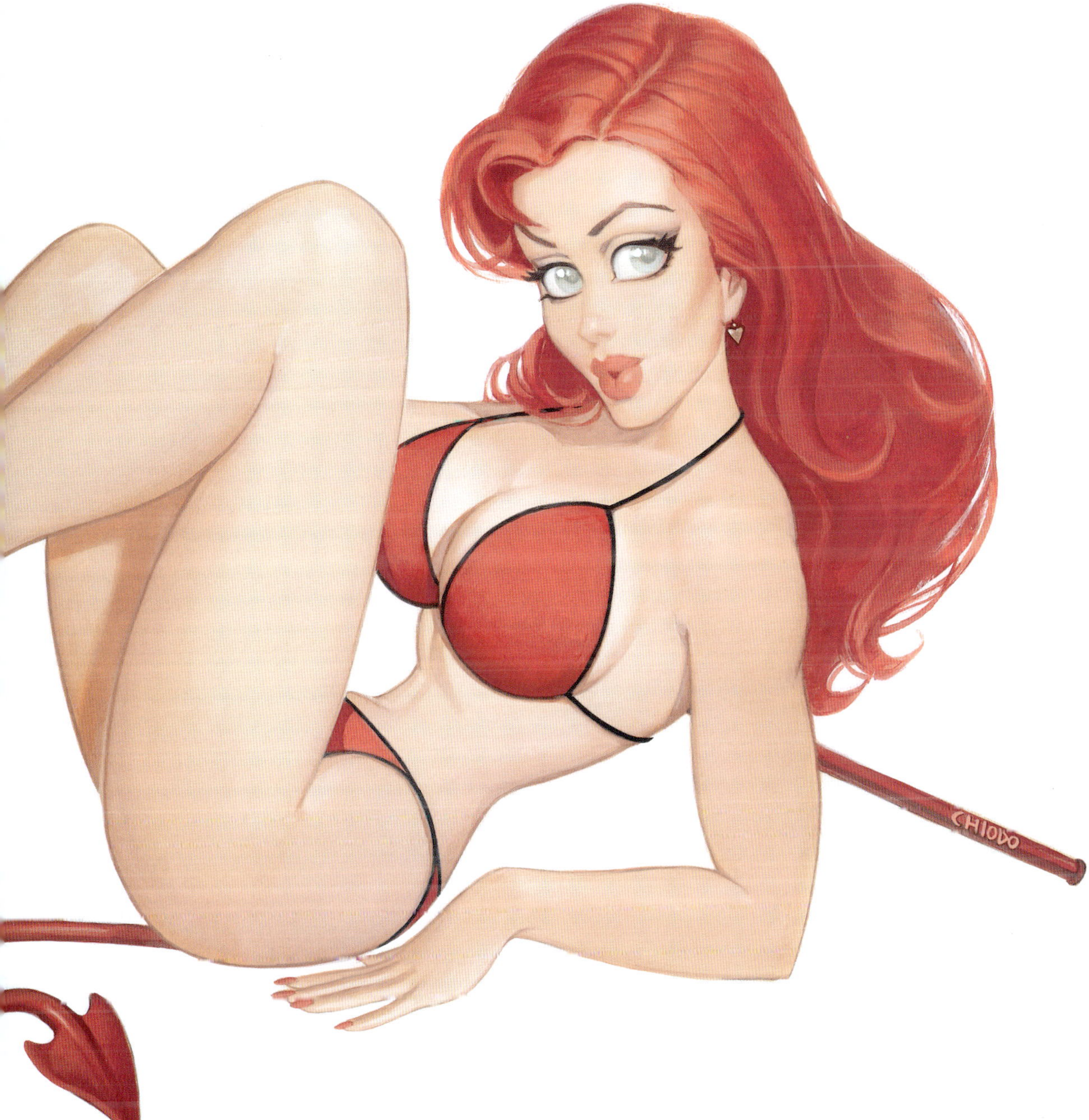
CHIODO

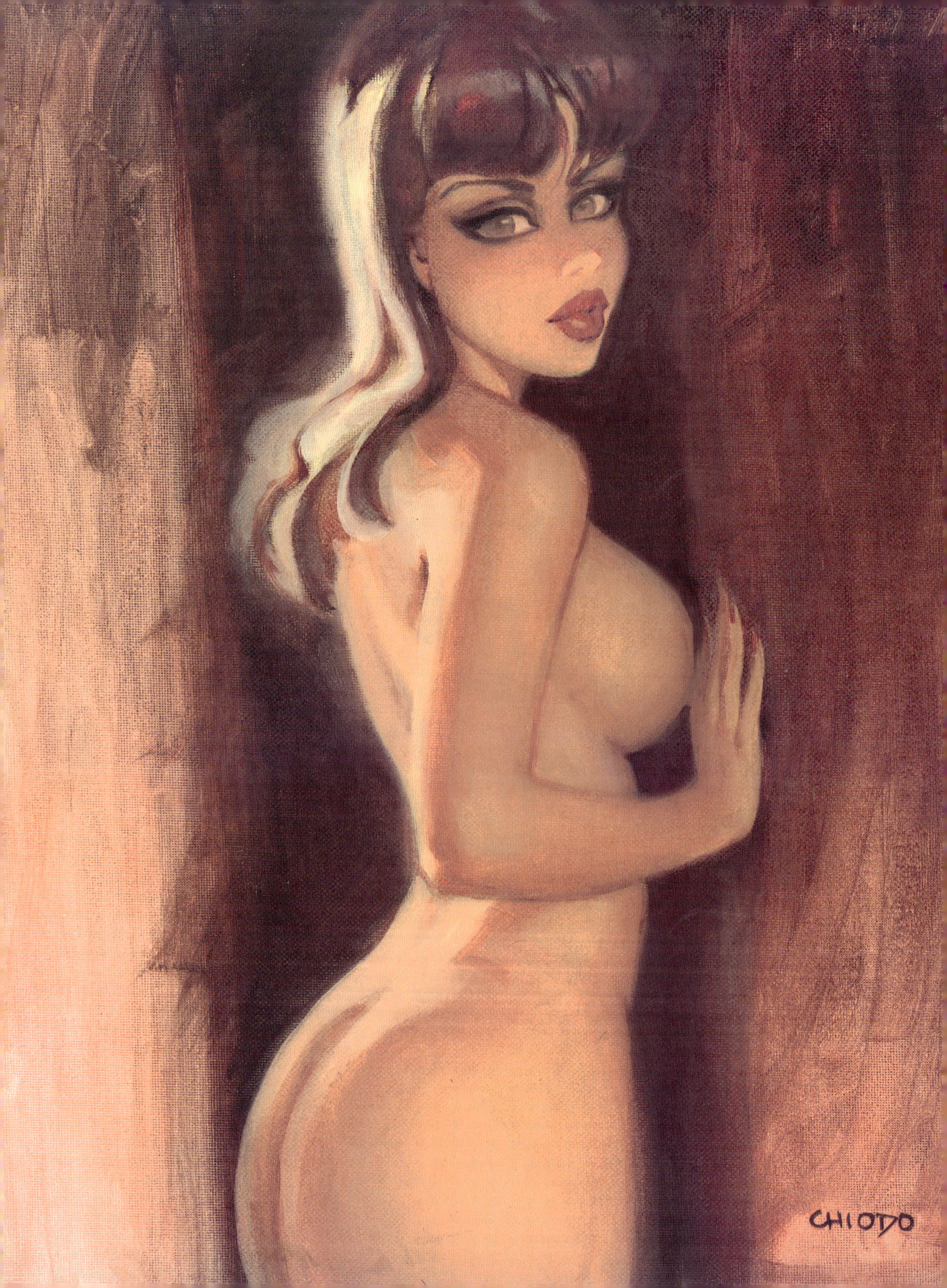
CHIODO

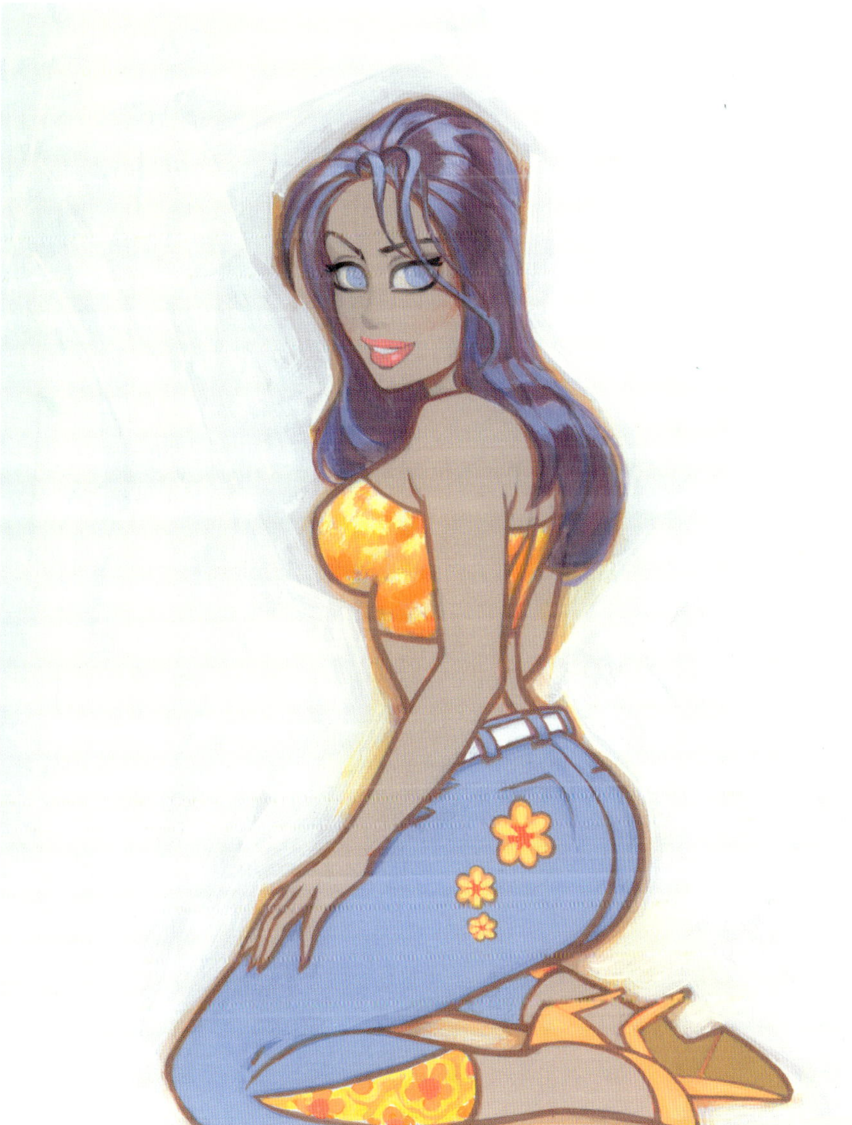

Opposite page: Turning, 2002, oil on board.
Above: Flowered Pants, 2002, acrylic on board.

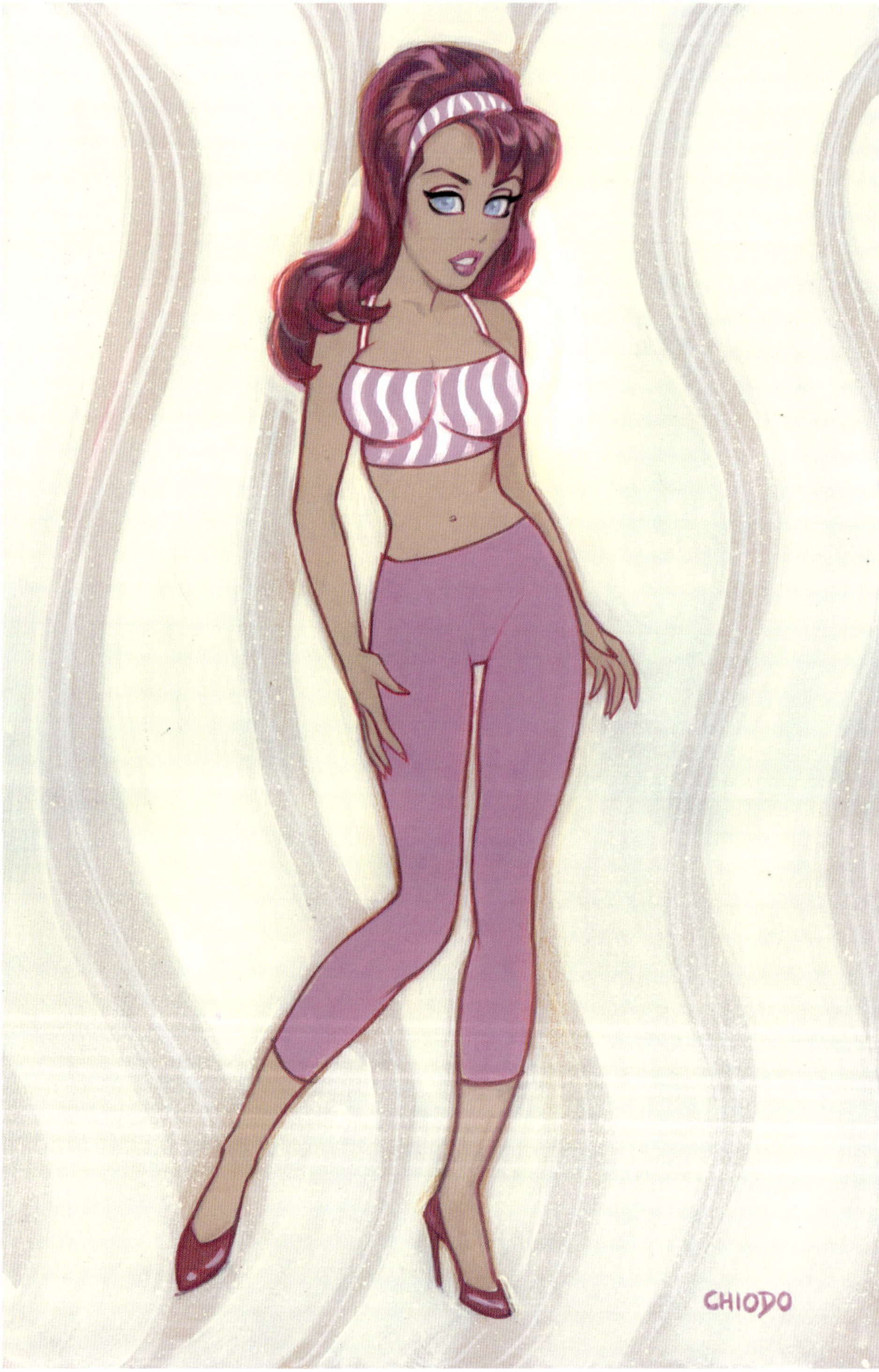

Pink Tights, 2002, acrylic on board

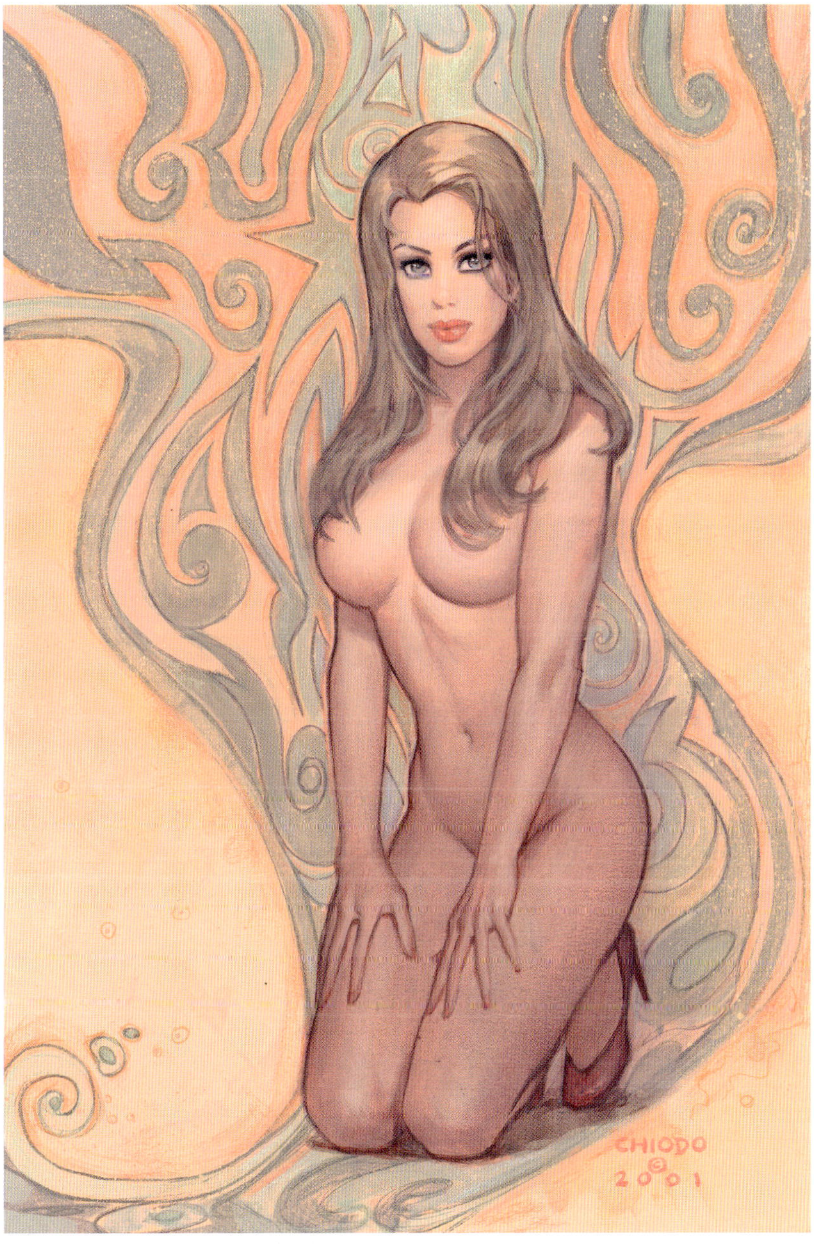

Psychedelic Aura, 2001, acrylic on board

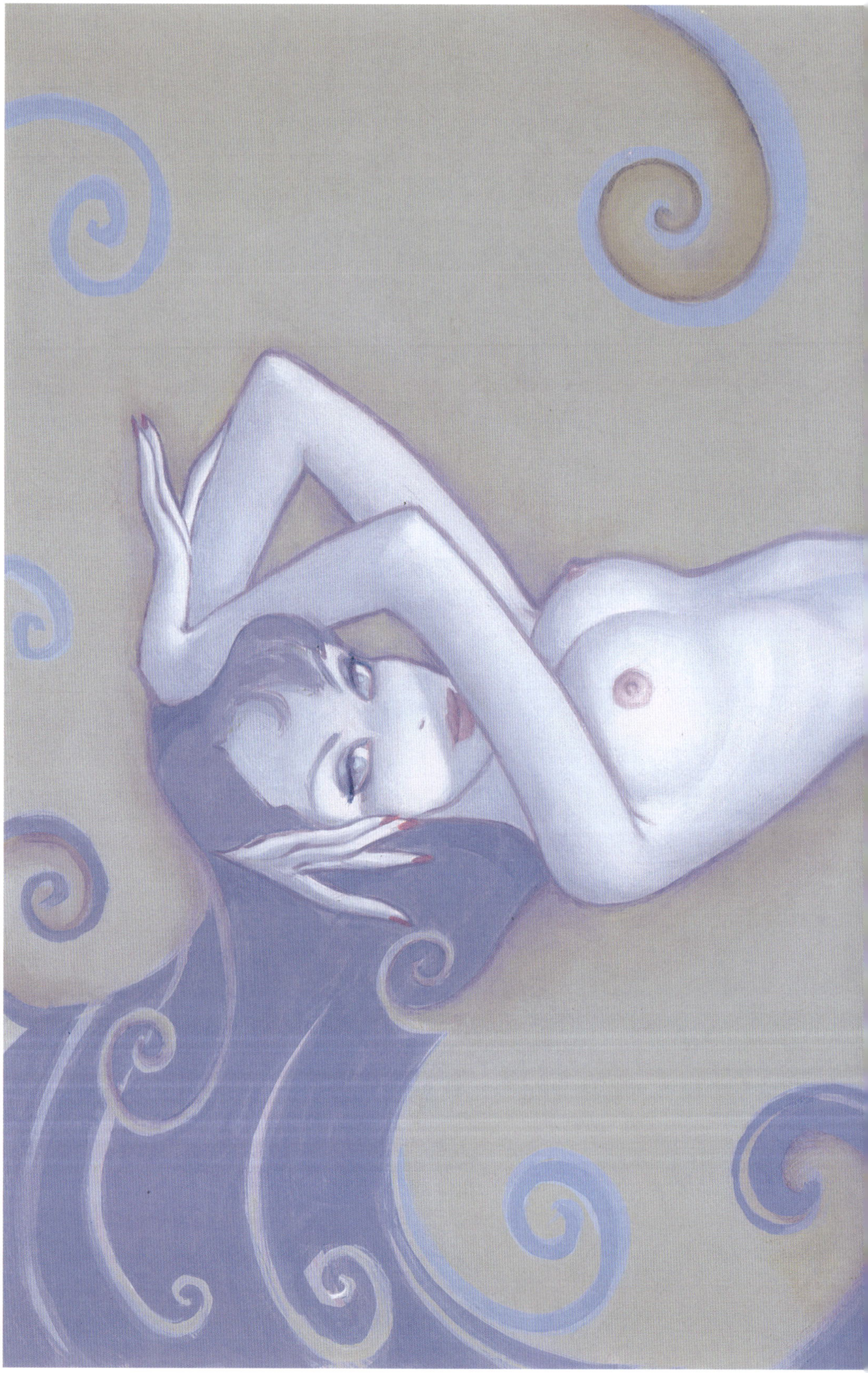

Spiral in Blue, 2002, acrylic and oil on board

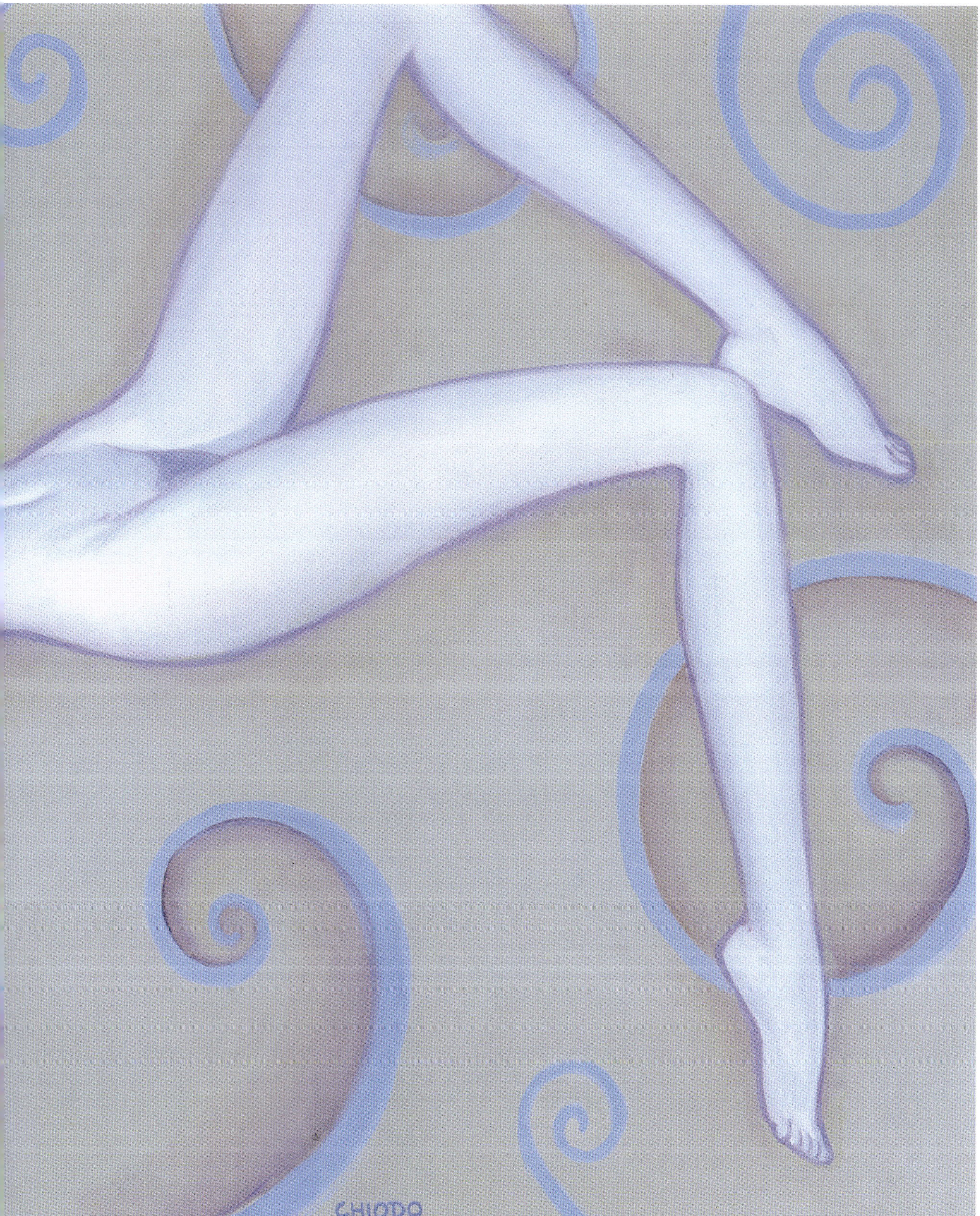
CHIODO

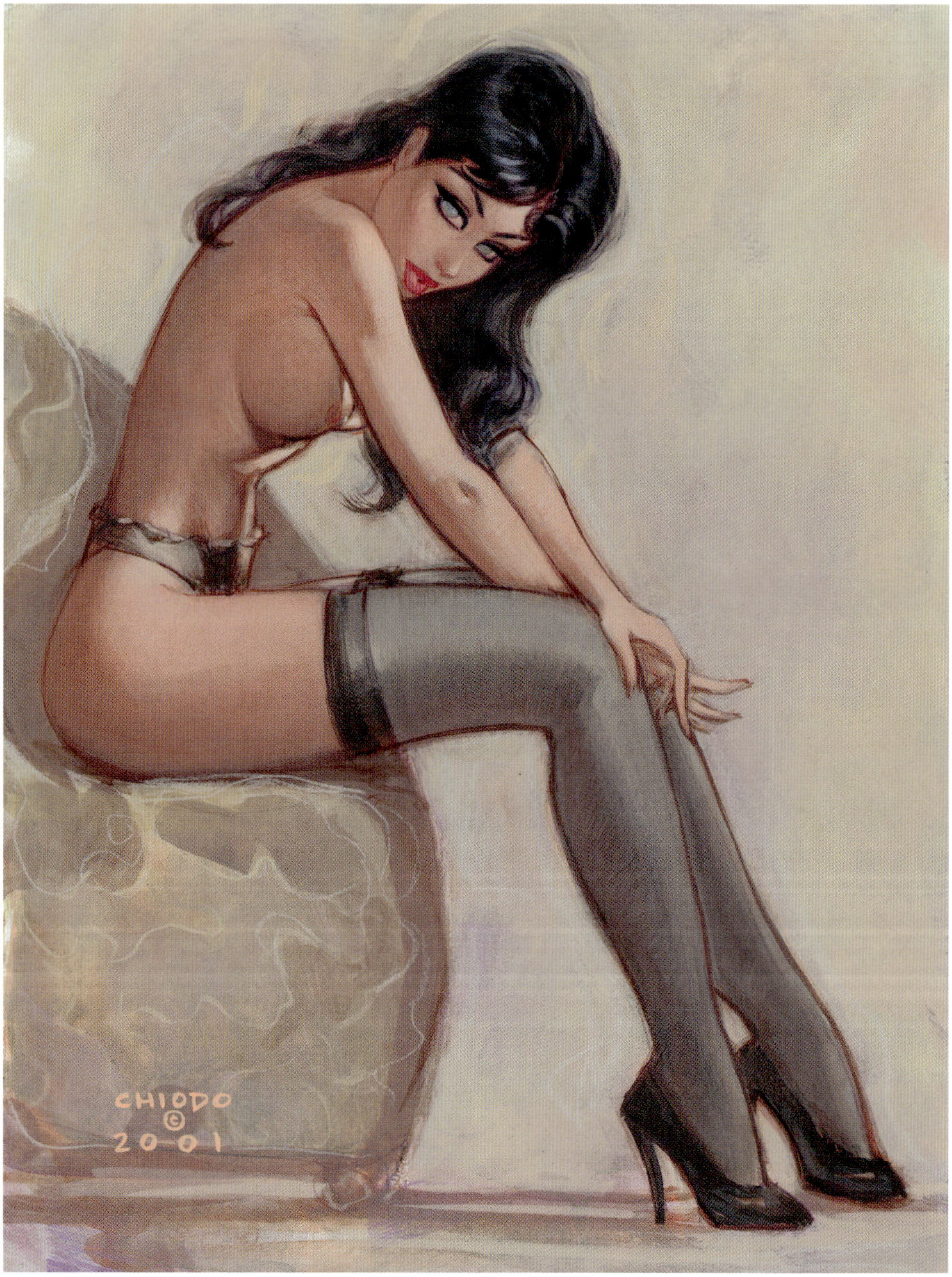

Above: Nylons, 2001, acrylic on board.
Opposite: Blood Cave, Vampirella cover, 2002, acrylic on board, ©2003 Harris Publications.

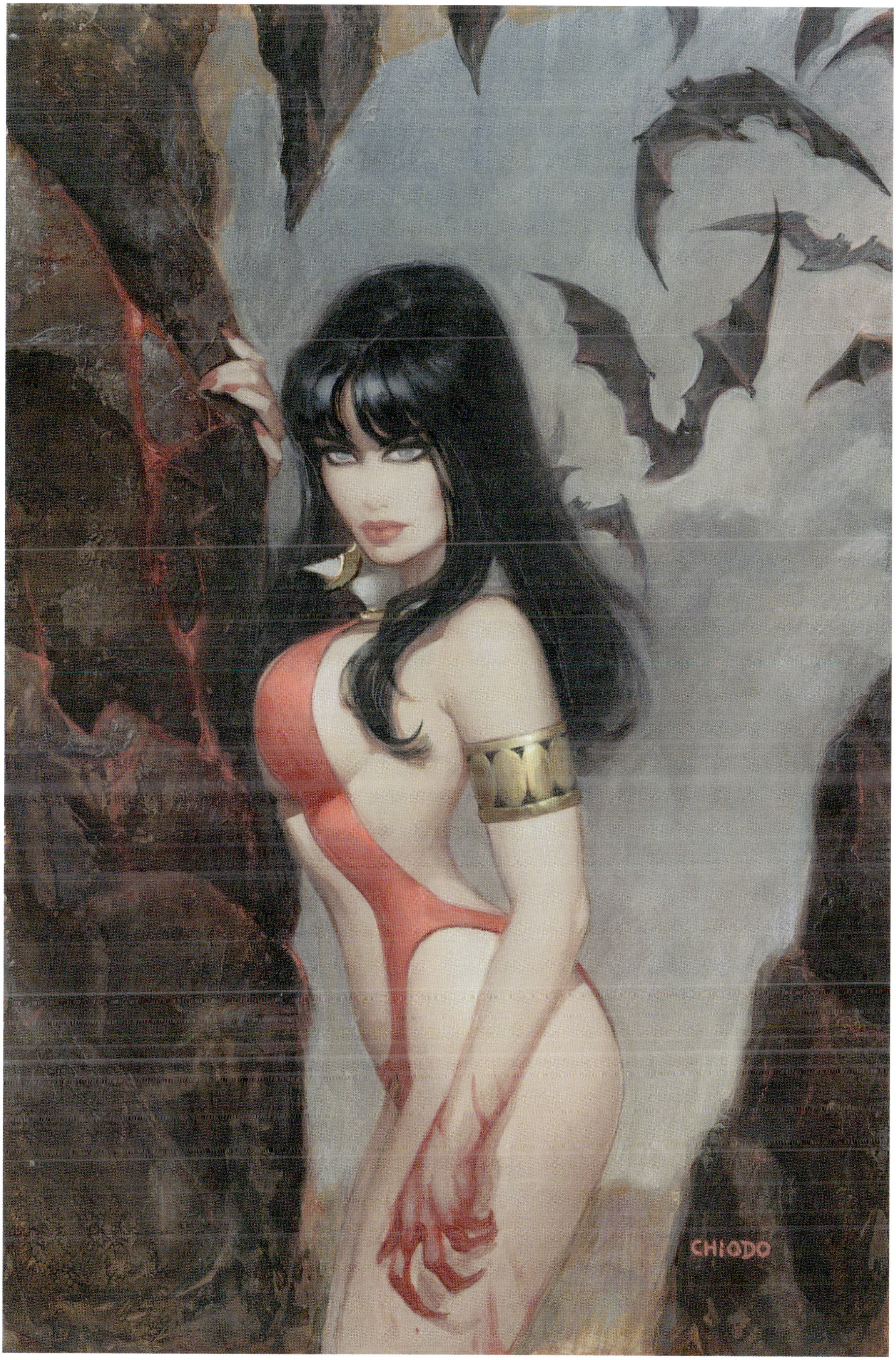
CHIODO

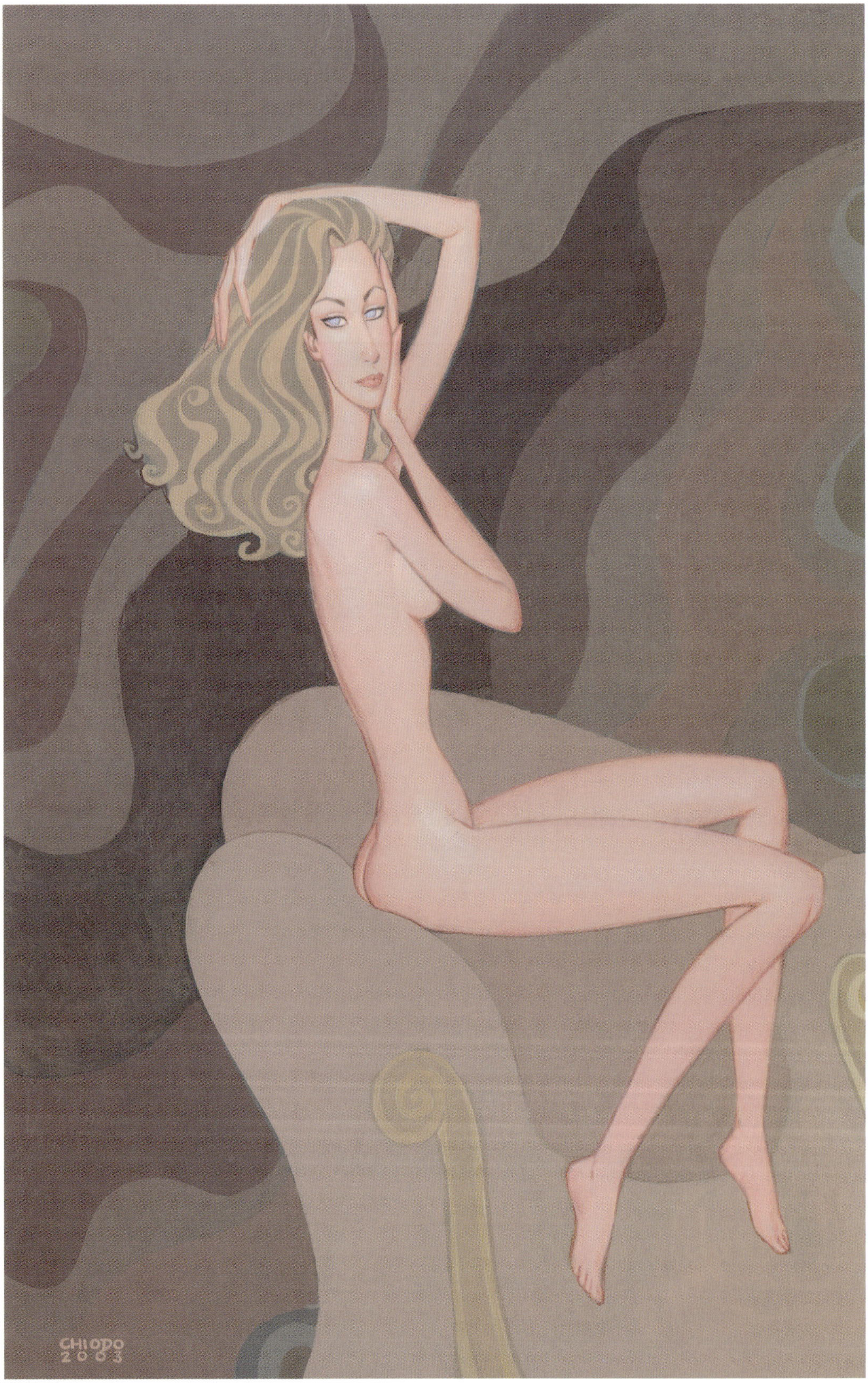

Adjustment, 2003, acrylic on board

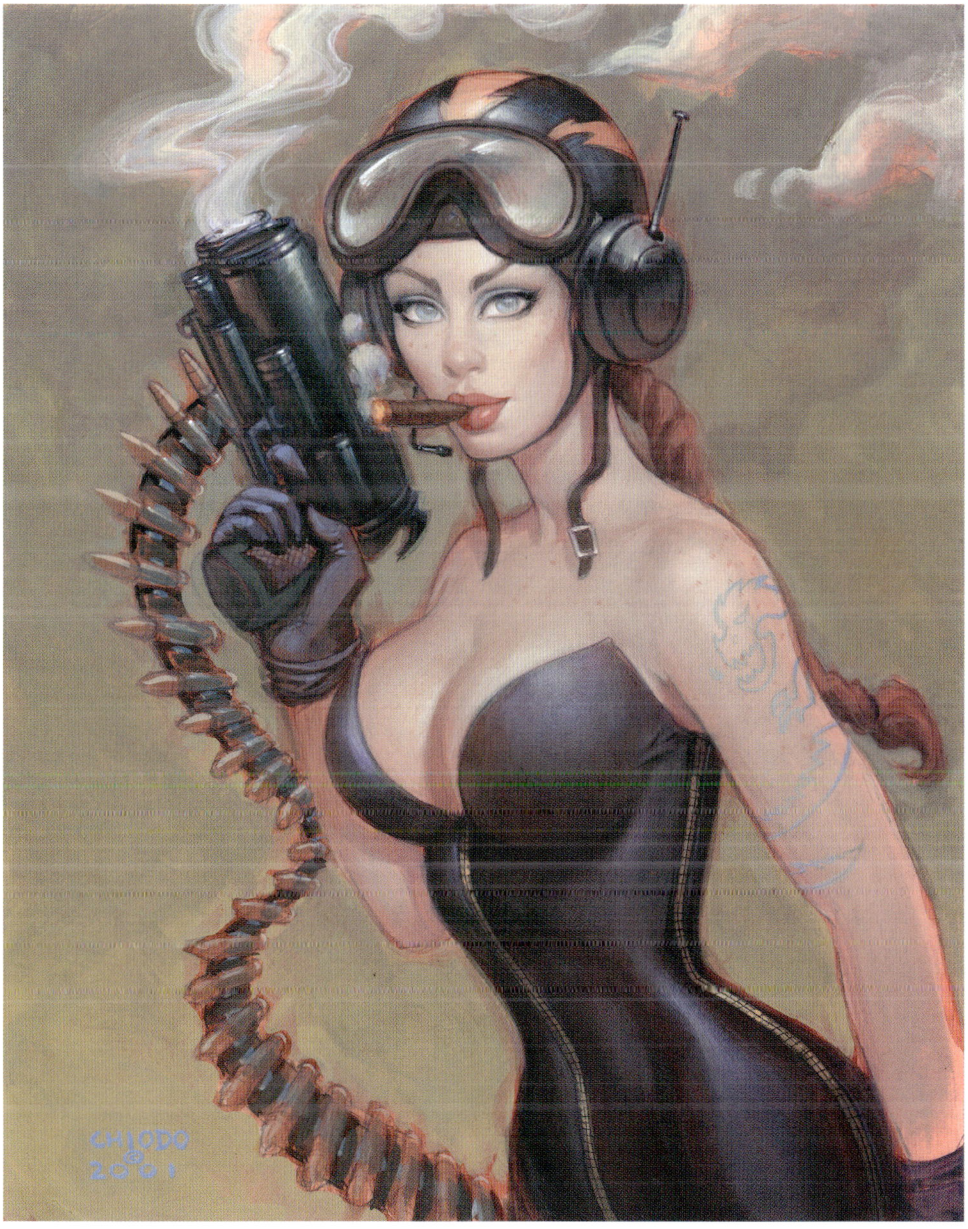

Gun Patrol, 2001, acrylic on board

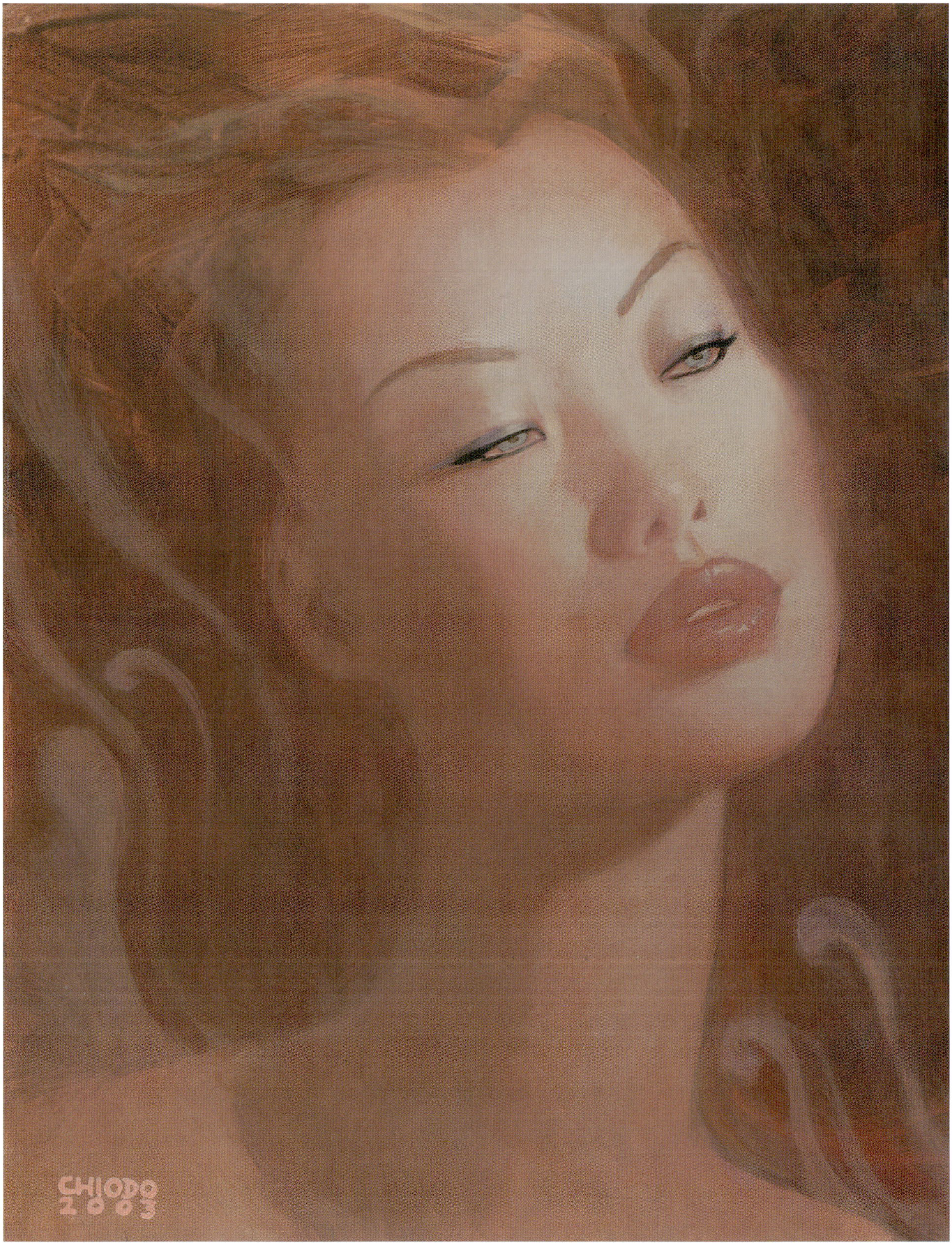

Above: Swirling Thoughts, 2003, acrylic on board.
Opposite: Swimming in Swirls, 2003, acrylic on board.

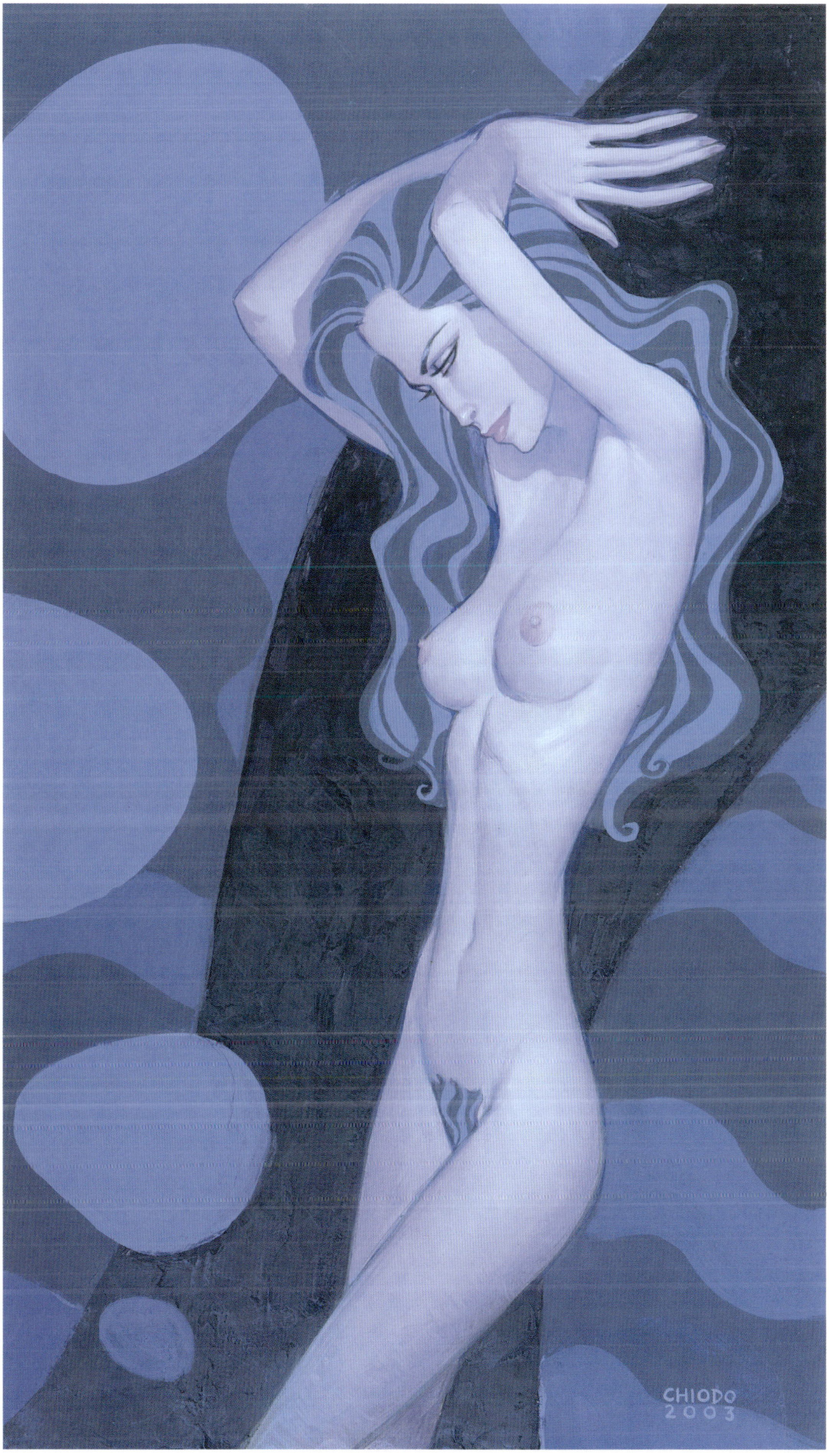
CHIODO
2003

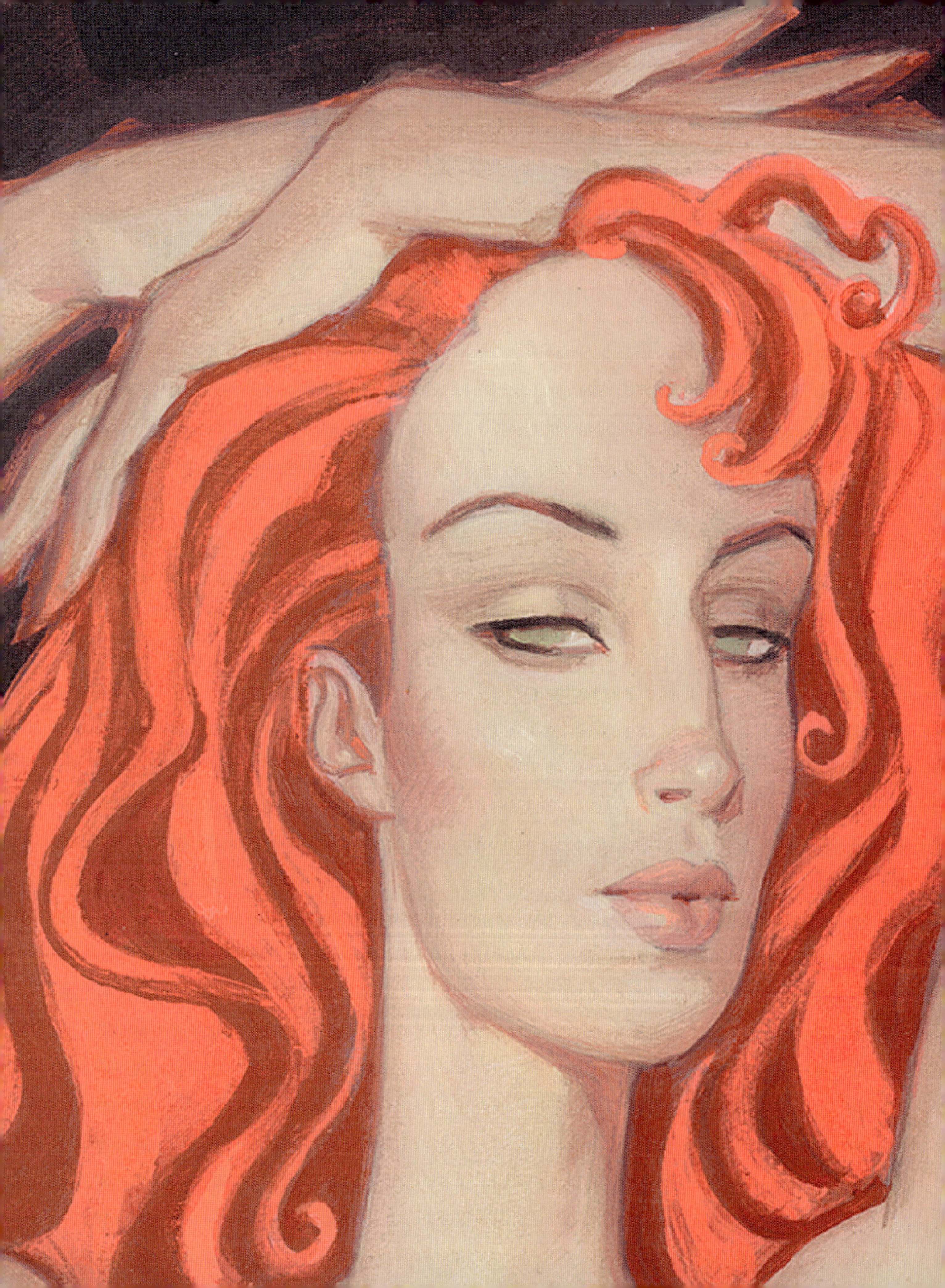

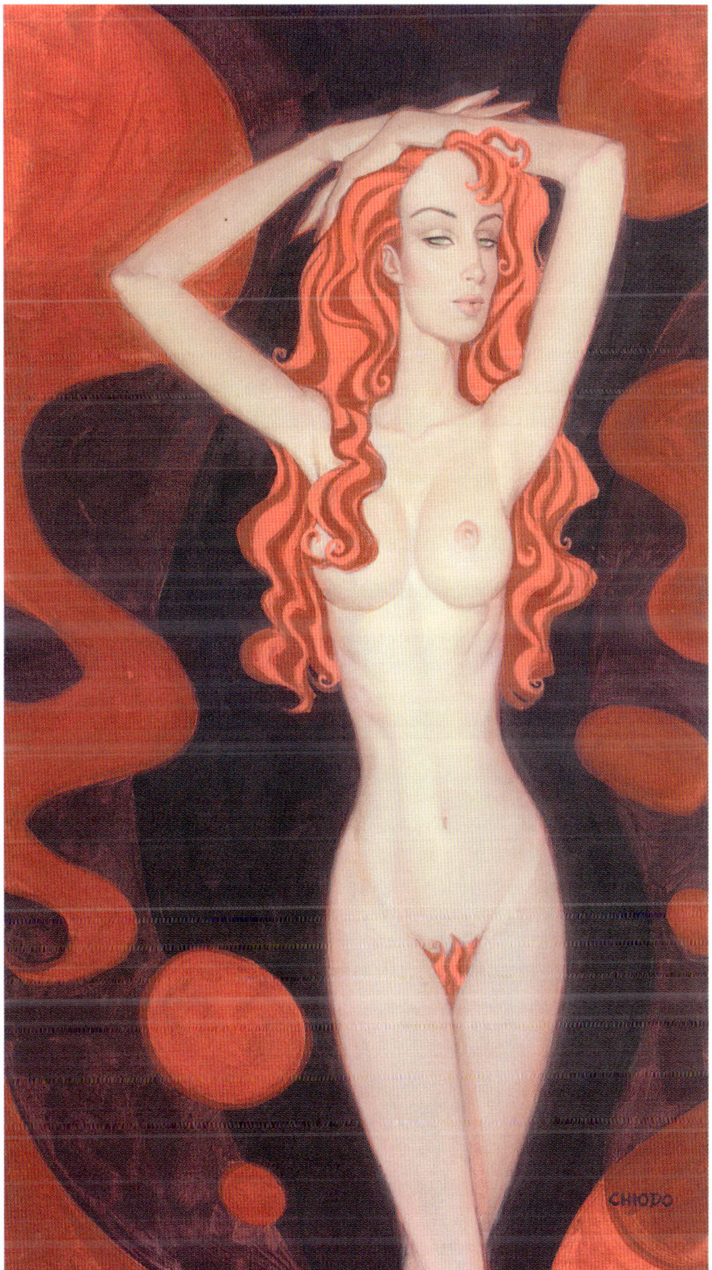

Lava Lamp, 2003, acrylic on board

THREE
COMICS

Comic strips and comic books have a long history of using seductive heroines and pretty women to attract the attention of readers. As early as the 1930s, Roy Crane was depicting partially unclad native girls and shapely women in his ground breaking strip, *Wash Tubbs*. Indeed, the great strips of the 1930s were populated with enticing women co-stars. Readers were attracted to Milton Caniff's *Terry and the Pirates* not only for exotic locales and adventure, but to see one of the most memorable characters of comic strips, the Dragon Lady. The talented and often overlooked Noel Sickles used attractive female characters with great style and effect in his pioneering strip, *Scorchy Smith*. Enchanting women drawn by talented artists have always populated the world of the comics. The pioneering strips of the 1930s all had important and attractive women characters, drawn in styles ranging from the looser cartoon style of *The Phantom* and *Dick Tracy* to the more illustrative style of Alex Raymond in *Flash Gordon* and Hal Foster in *Prince Valiant*.

The birth of comic books soon witnessed the creation of male and female superheroes along with casts of characters featuring handsome men and engaging women. Unfortunately, many of the early artists in comic books were not accomplished cartoonists or illustrators. There were, however, some noteworthy exceptions. Will Eisner's *Spirit,* which premiered in 1940, boasted beautifully drawn women characters, who, even after sixty years still merit a wink and a smile. After the end of World War II, a whole new generation of artists came on the scene who added more than just a little spice to the women in comic books. Matt Baker, Lee Elias, Frank Frazetta, and Wally Wood are but a few noteworthy examples of the talented artists who came into the medium at that time. The work of Chiodo fits firmly in this tradition with an exception, he is able to fully paint his characters, whereas prior generations of artists were limited to pencilling and inking their work only to have it colored by others. The work in this chapter ranges from pencil preliminary work to three pages of an unpublished comic book story. The artwork, as with the rest of this book, is diverse and amply demonstrates Chiodo's many dimensions as an artist.

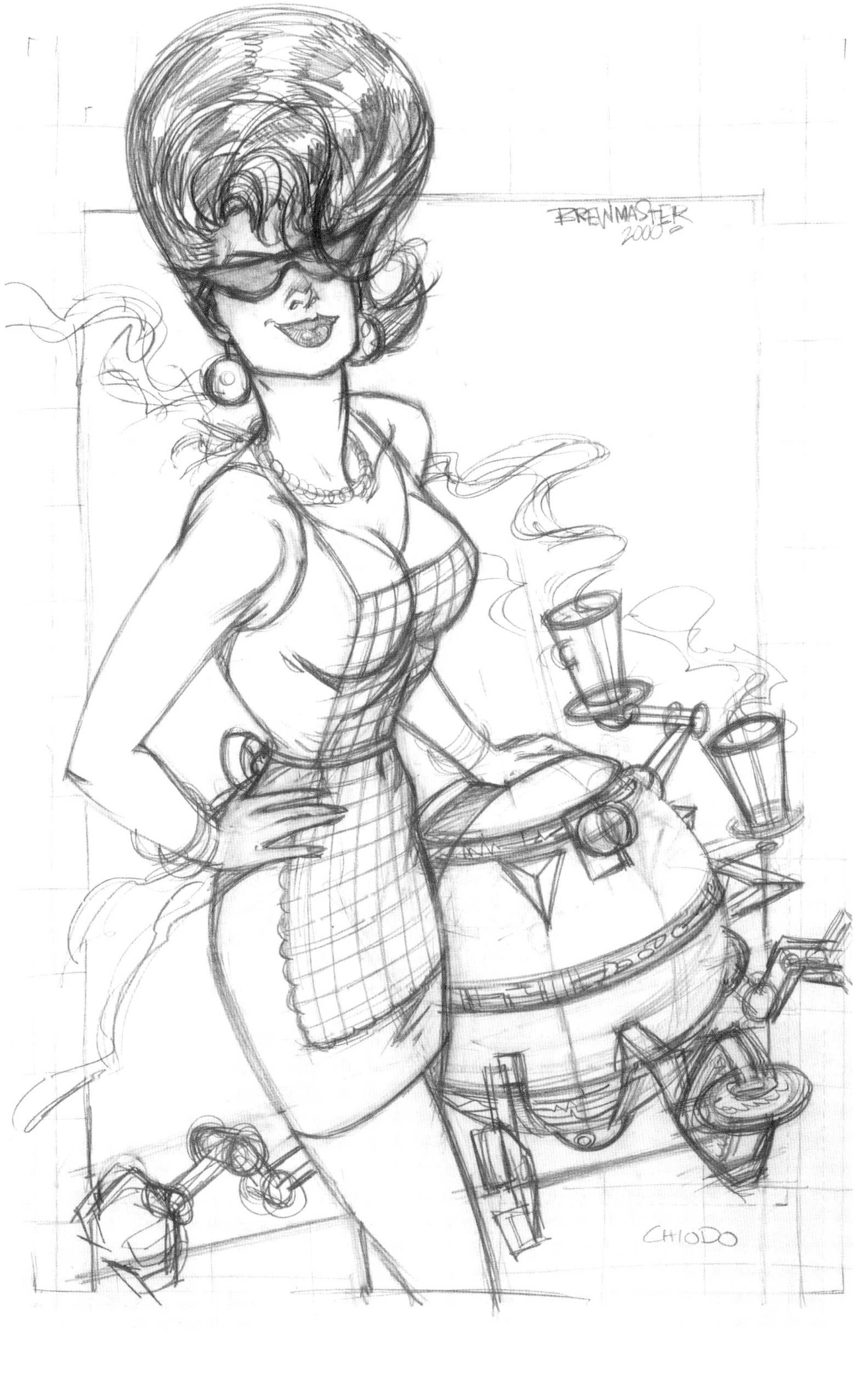

Brewmaster 2000 Preliminary, 1996, pencil on paper

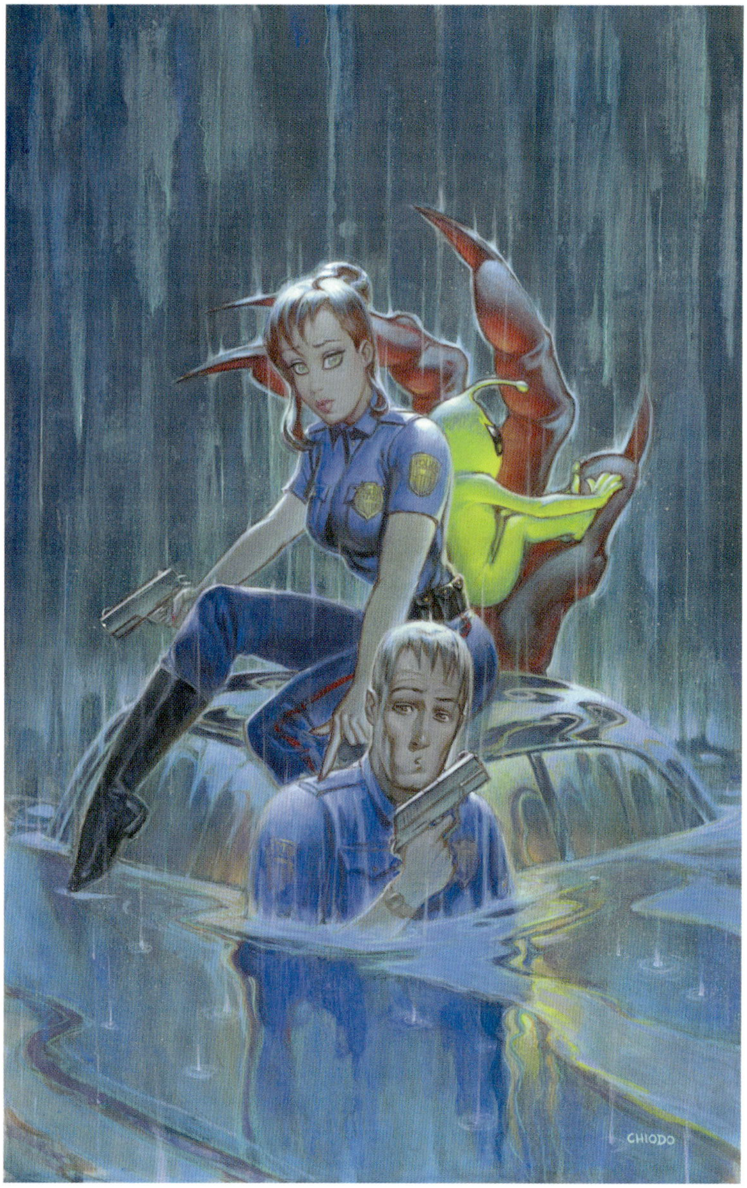

Above: Rising Tide, *Decoy*, 2002, acrylic on board, ©2003 Penny Farthing Press. Right: Bottled Up, *Decoy*, 2002, acrylic on board, ©2003 Penny Farthing Press.

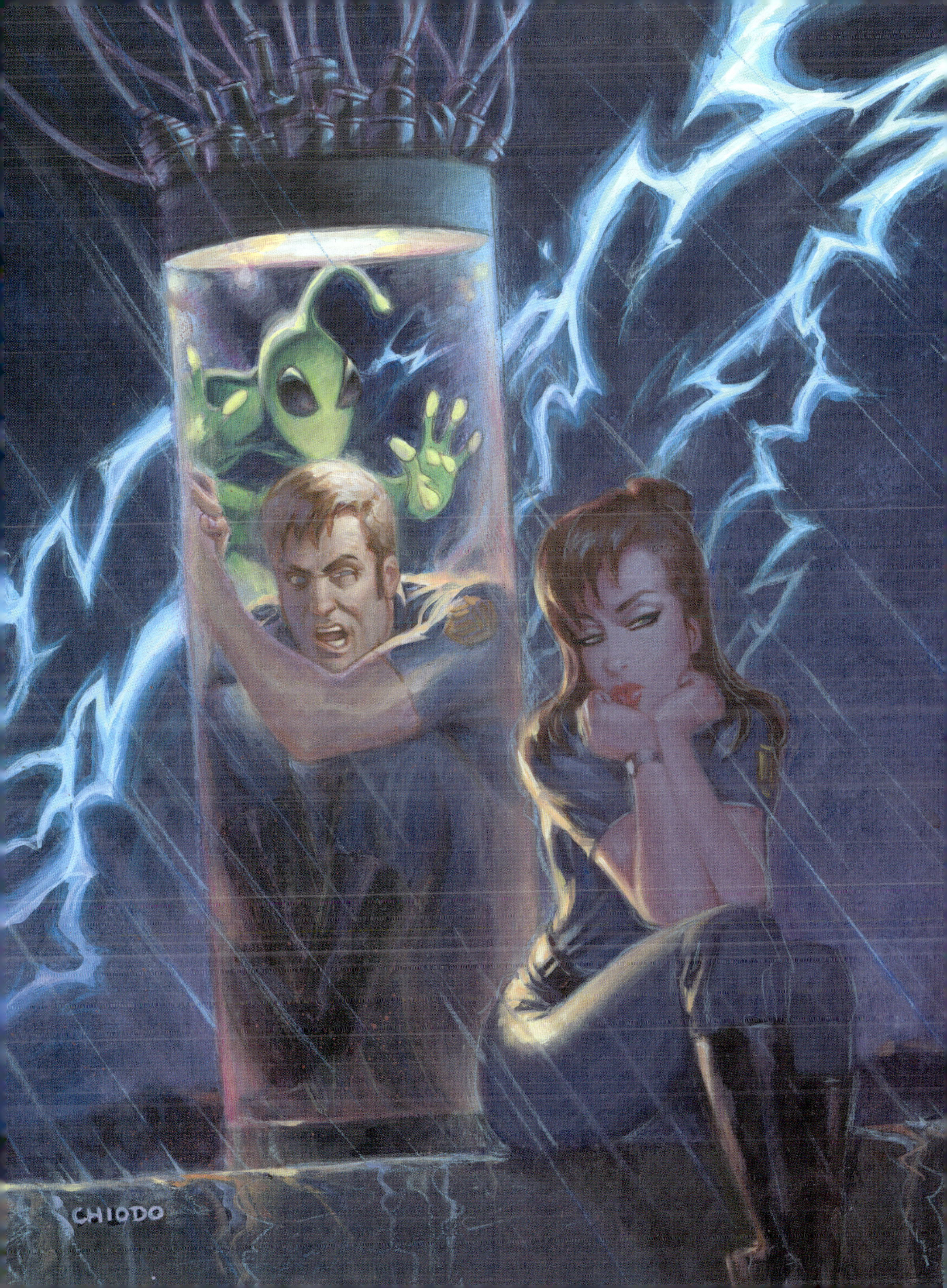
CHIODO

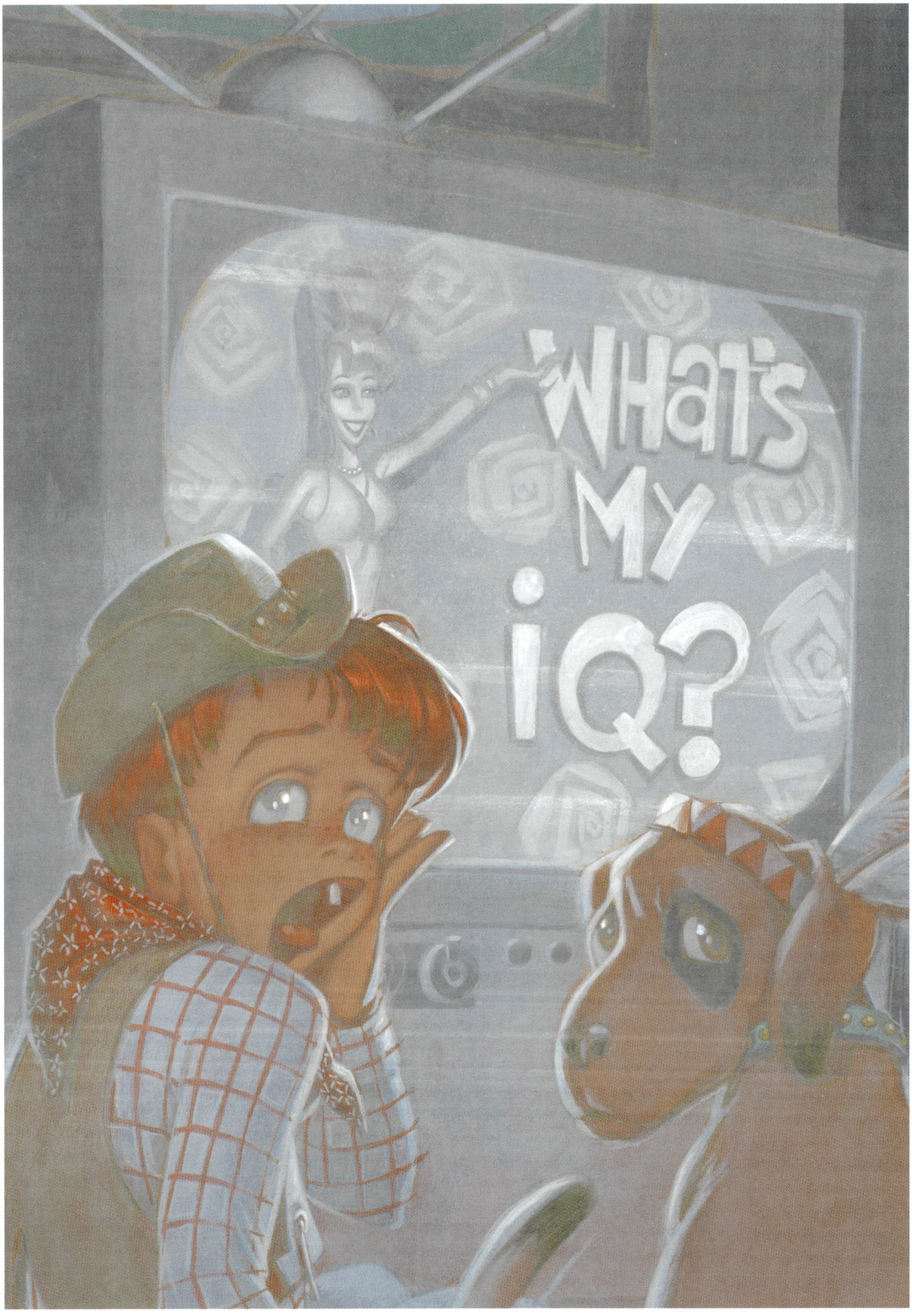
WHAT'S
MY
IQ?

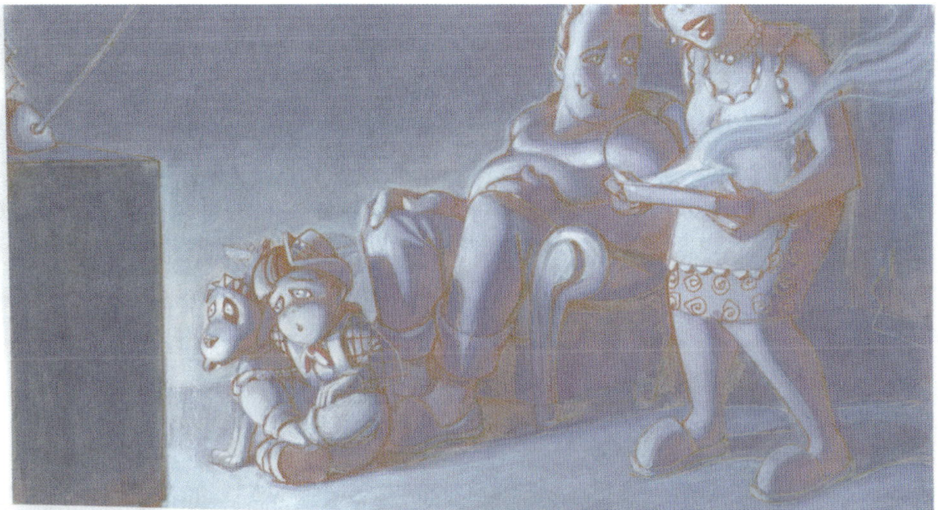

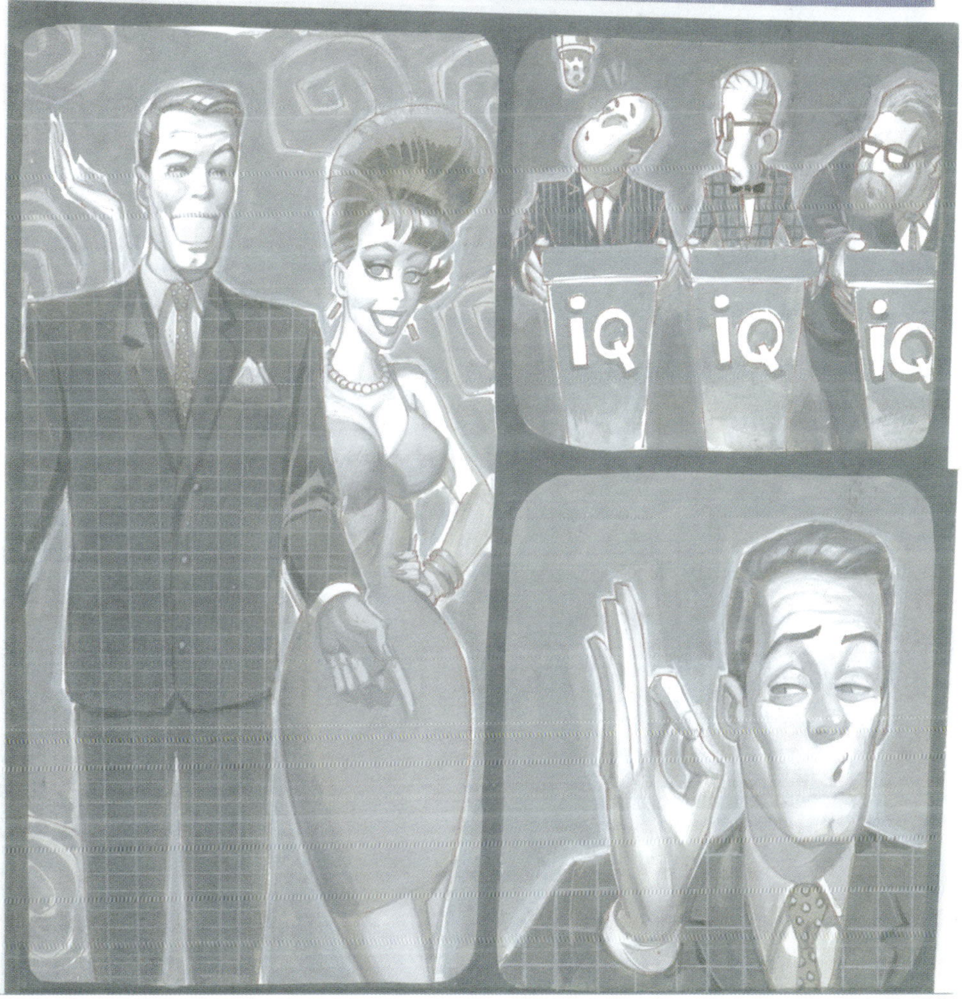

Opposite page, above, and the next page, *What's My IQ?*, original unpublished story, 2002, acrylic, markers, and pencil on paper. These three pages were done as a pitch for a larger story which is yet to be finished. There is no dialogue but the storytelling in this three page continuity is clear and clever and only hints at what might be in store. Hopefully, someday Chiodo will complete work on this story.

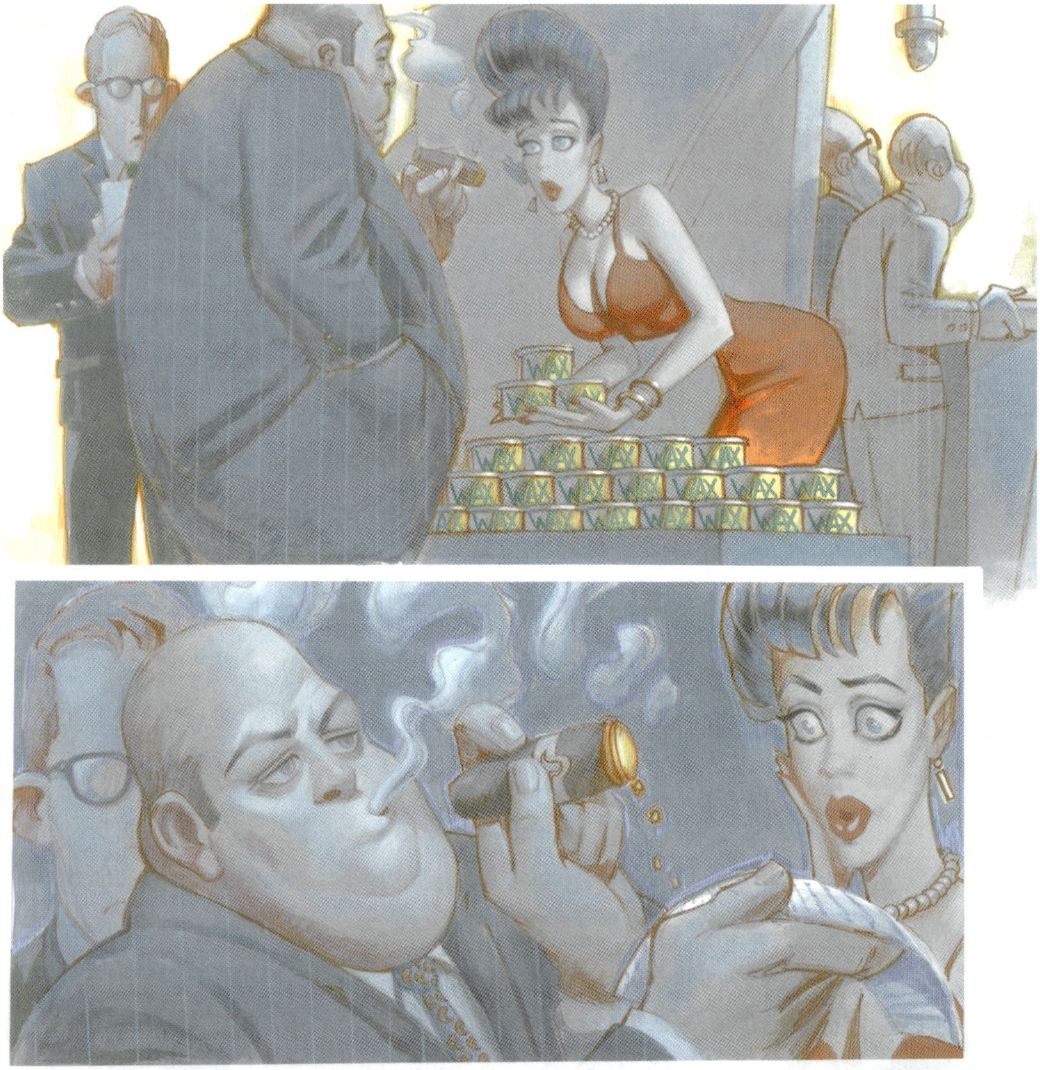
WAX
STUDIO B

This page and pages 62 through 65 contain model sheets for various games and character designs.

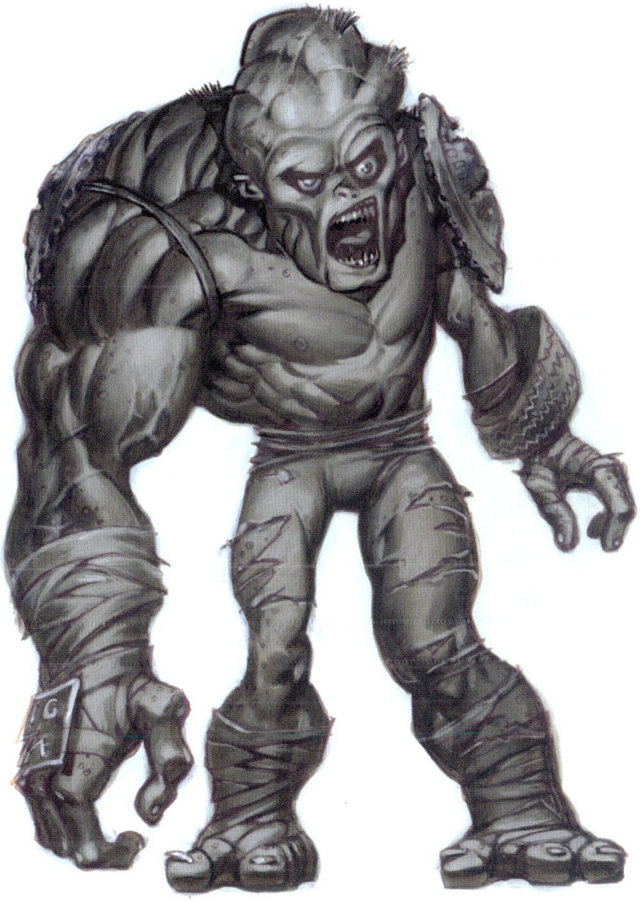

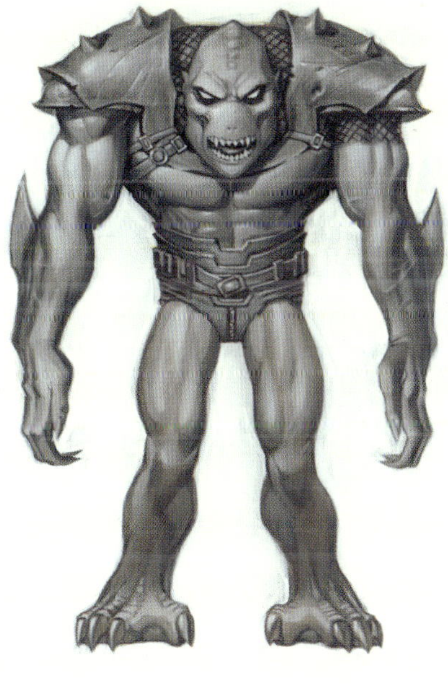

Top: Trashman, 1999, acrylic on paper.
Bottom: Brutus, 1999, acrylic on paper.

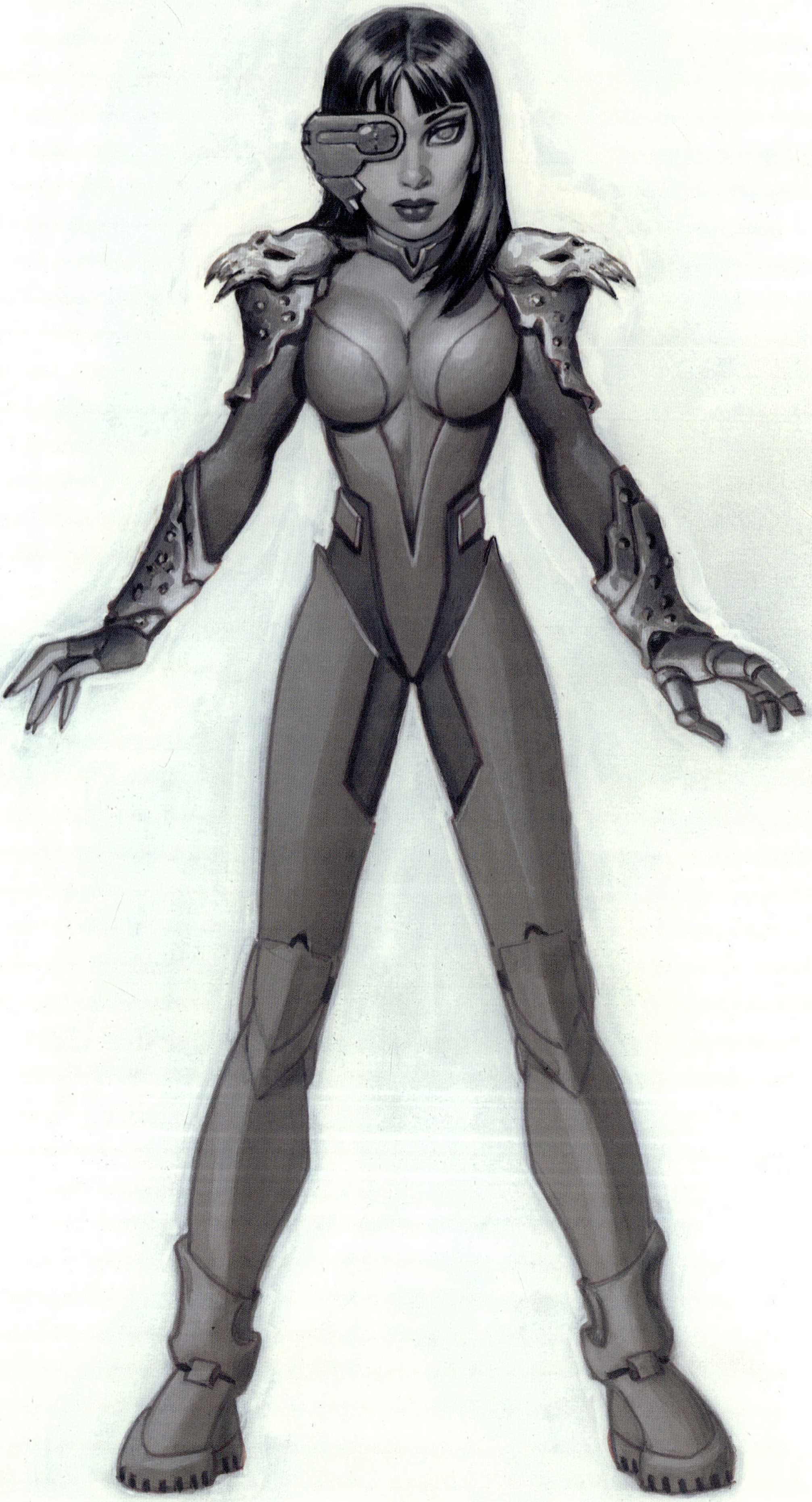

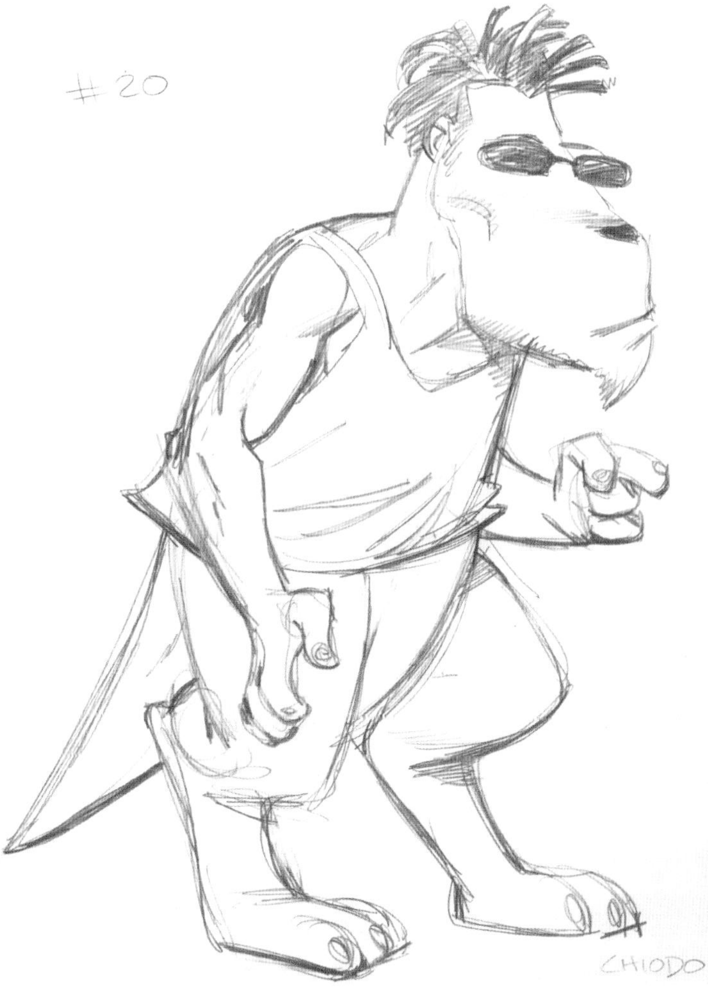

Opposite page: Sniper, 1999, acrylic on paper.
Top: Electronic Arts #20, 1999, pencil on paper.
Bottom: Electronic Arts #18, 1999, pencil on paper.

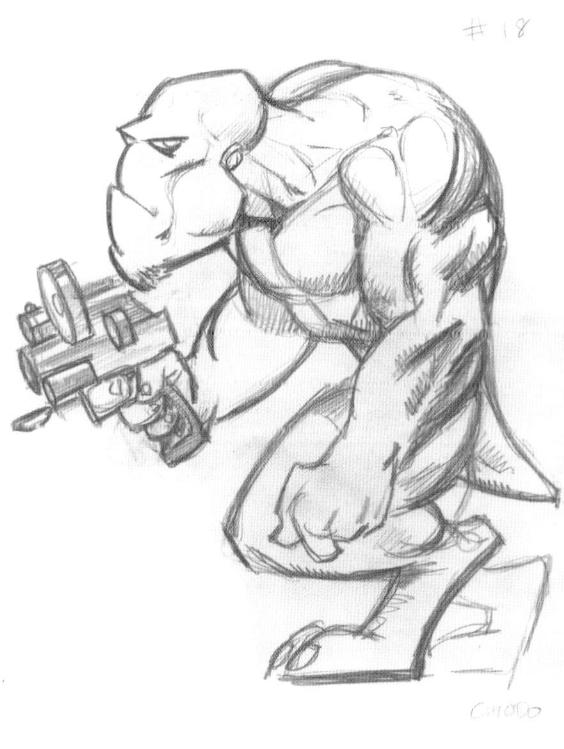

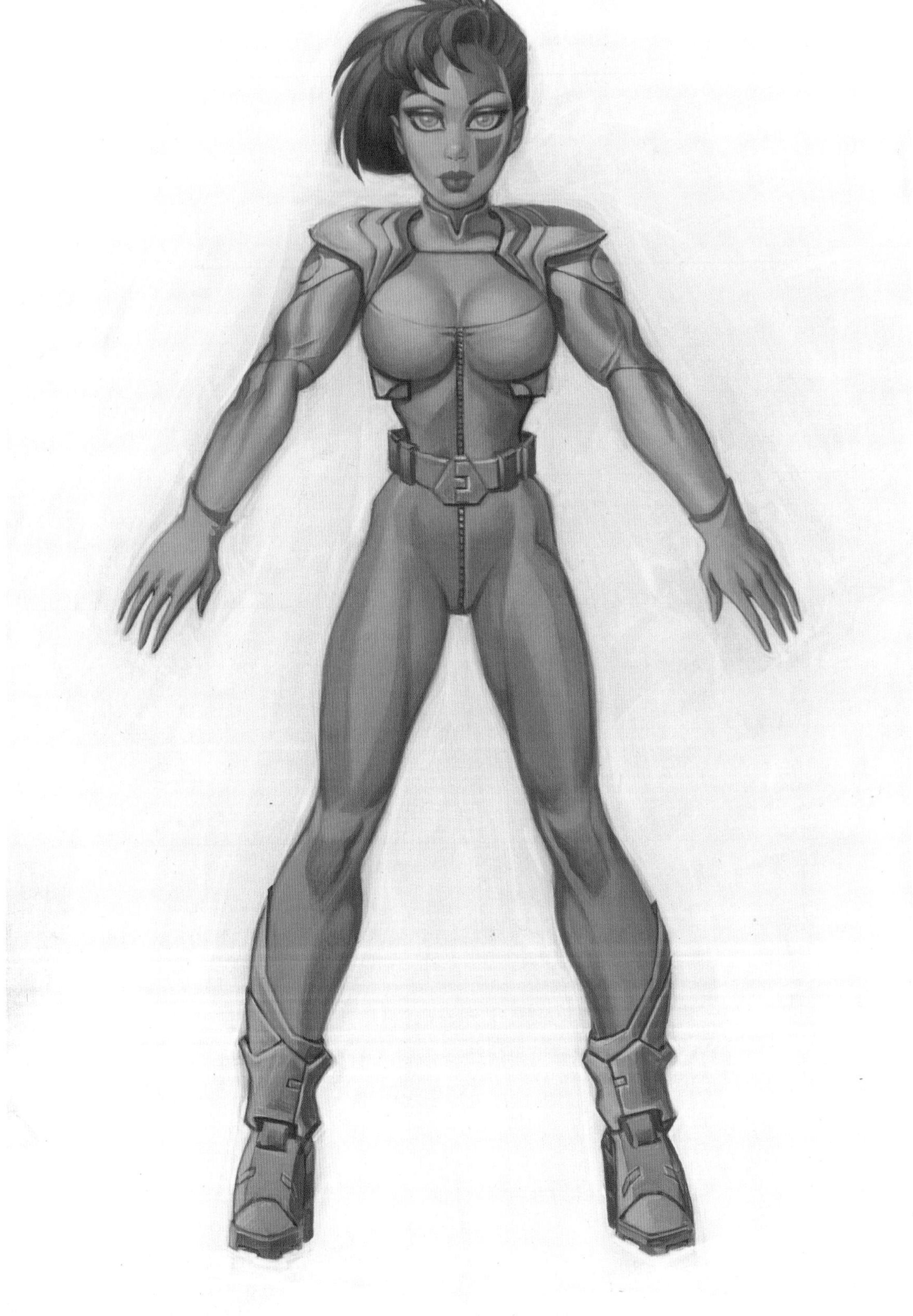

Scout, 1999, acrylic on paper

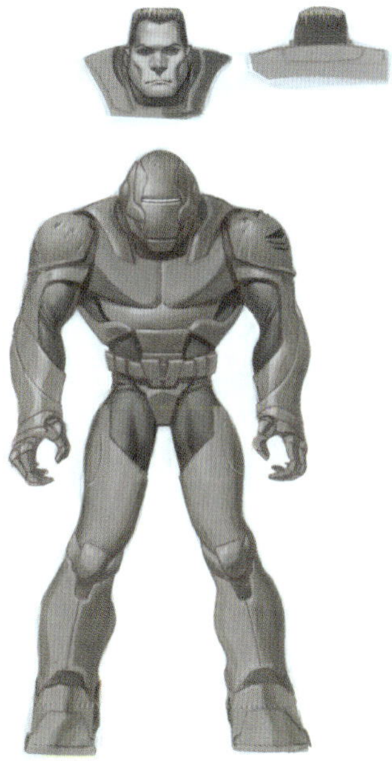

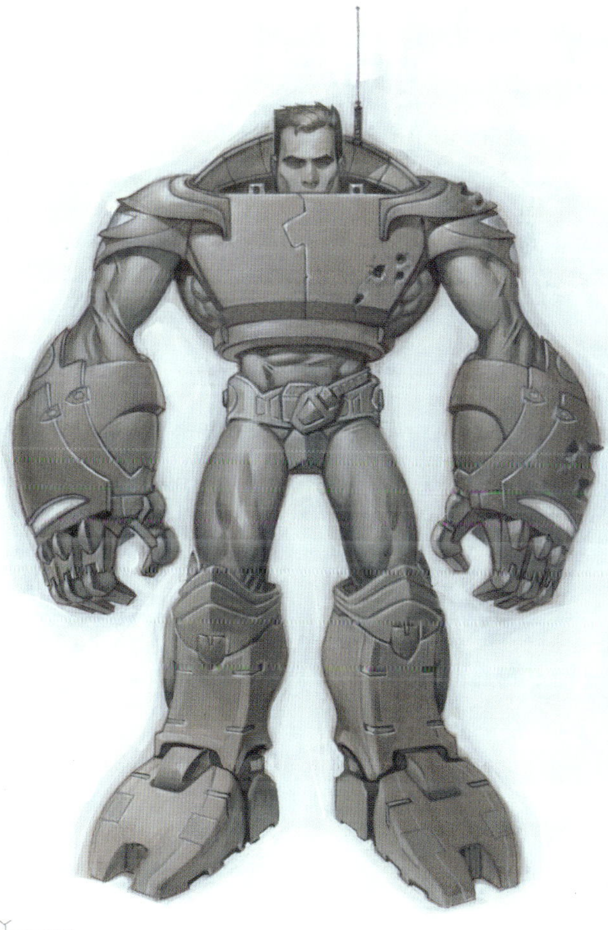

Top: Militia, 1999, acrylic on paper.
Bottom: Kilroy, 1999, acrylic on paper.

FOUR

PAINTING

Chiodo has always alternated between painting figures in a cartoon or "big foot" style and working purely as an illustrator. He is not limited to working within the confines of one genre and freely moves back and forth, depicting subjects requiring the simplified language of the cartoon to a more painterly style.

No matter what the style, however, the artwork is always unmistakably his. The final chapter of this book, *Painting*, amply demonstrates how easily Chiodo steps from the vernacular of the cartoon and the comic book, to the language of the contemporary pin-up, to figure painting and landscapes. The paintings in this chapter are depicted in a broad range of tones which Chiodo uses less frequently in his pin-ups, but make no mistake about it, many of the paintings presented in this section are extraordinarily effective as pin-ups. Also on view are several landscapes and some very sensitive portraiture.

Chiodo is by no means the only artist associated with comic books to work in a diverse number of media and styles. Many of the most distinguished comic strip and comic book artists spent large portions of their careers working in illustration art, advertising art, and painting. The paintings and illustrations of artists primarily associated with comic books are seldom seen, however. This, fortunately is not the case here, as Chiodo's work is on full display in this chapter.

For the last two years, Chiodo has spent much of his time teaching and painting. He has, as this book documents, continued to paint pin-ups and work on comic book art. He has also, as we see by the number of figure studies in this chapter, continued to hone his skill as a colorist and a painter.

Posturing, 2001, acrylic on board

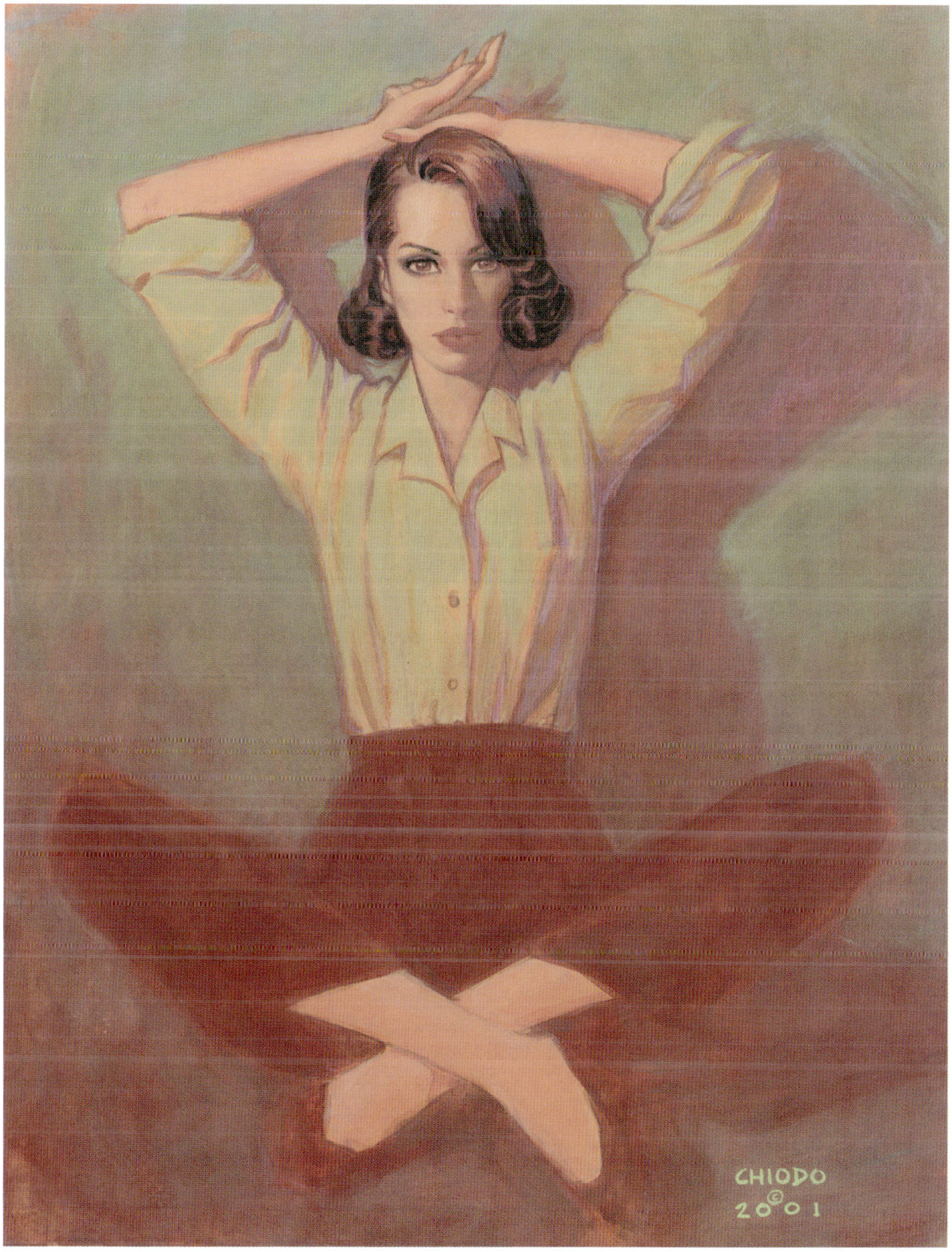

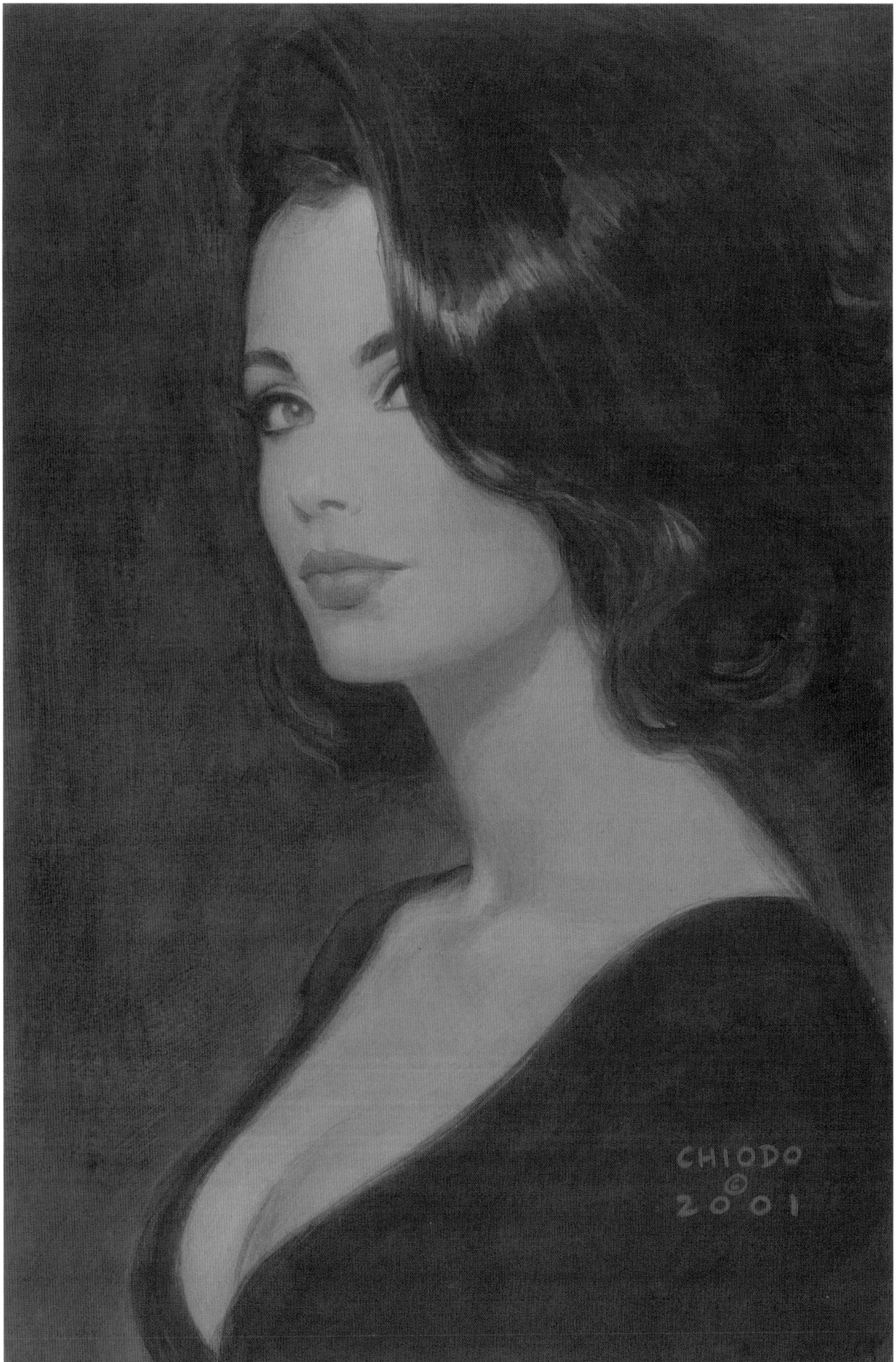

Black Dress, 2001, acrylic on board

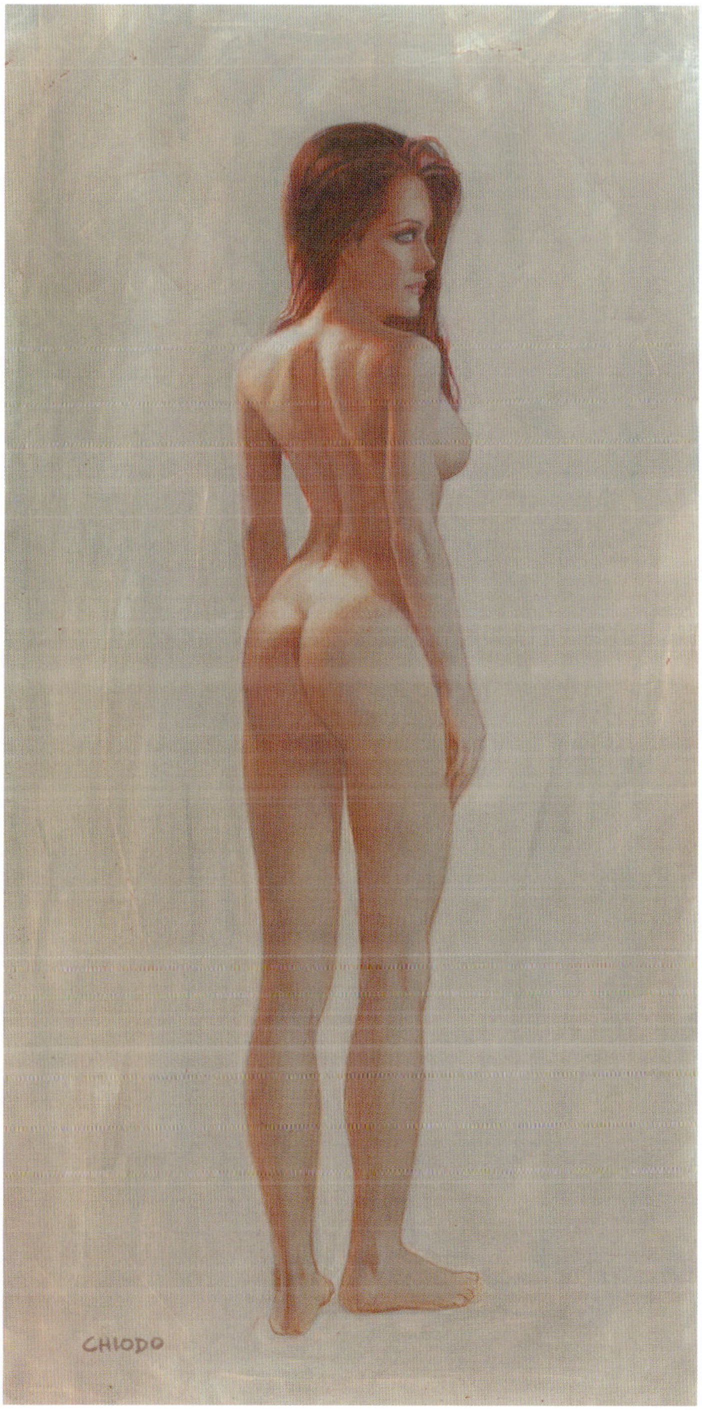

Big Head Chick, 2002, acrylic on board

Below: Back Study, 2001, oil on canvas.
Right: Nude in Purple, 2002, acrylic on board.

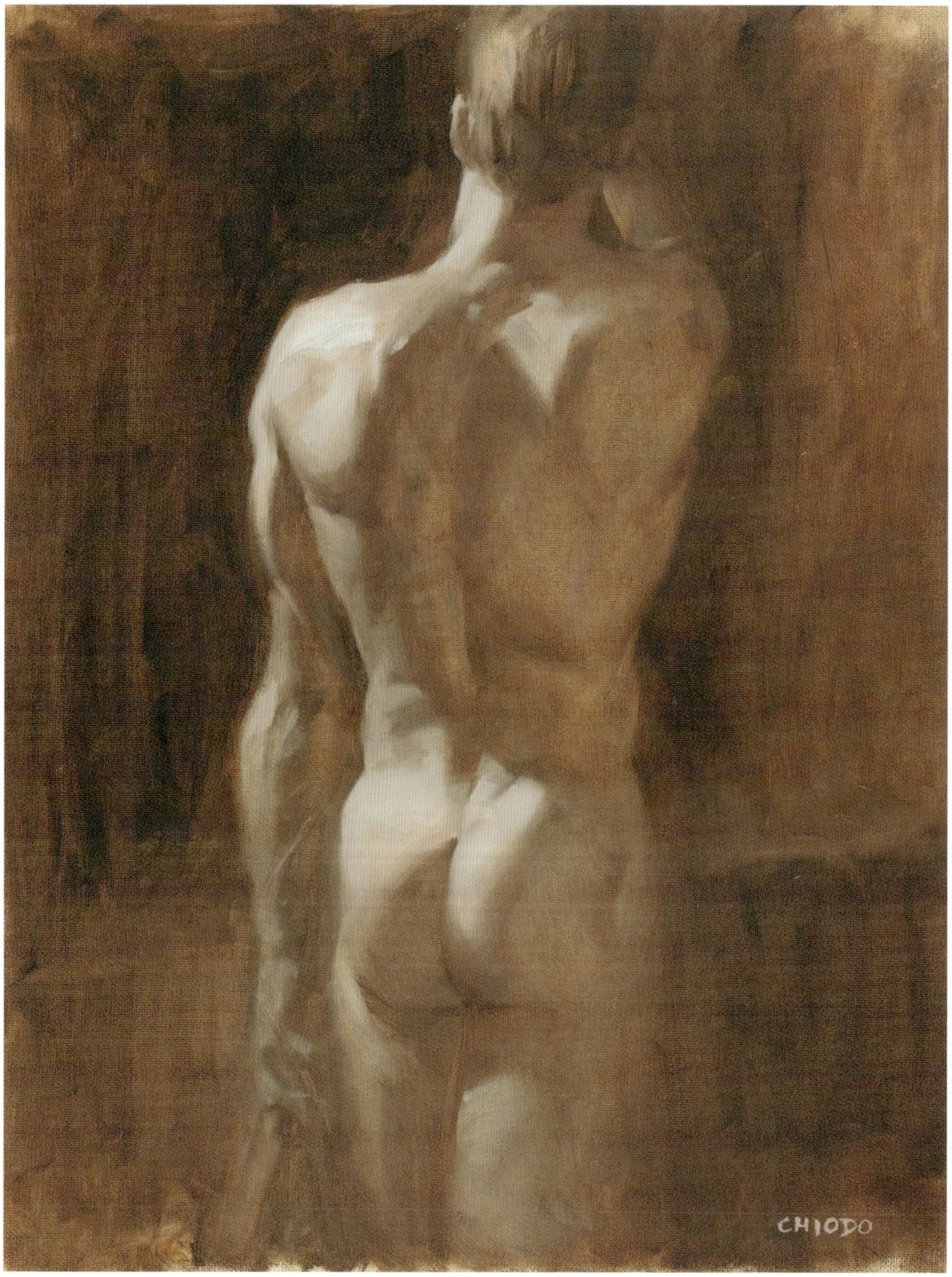

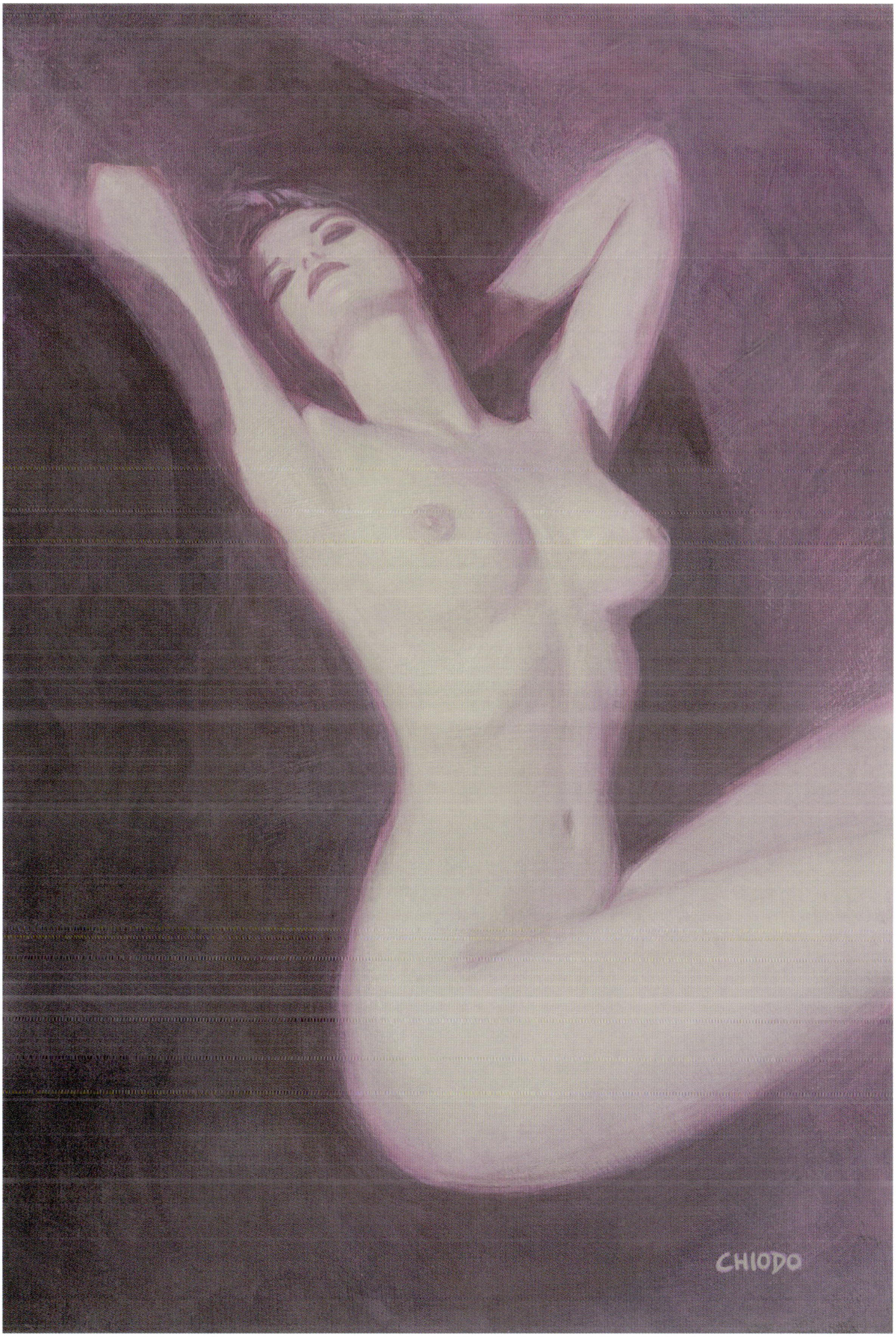
CHIODO

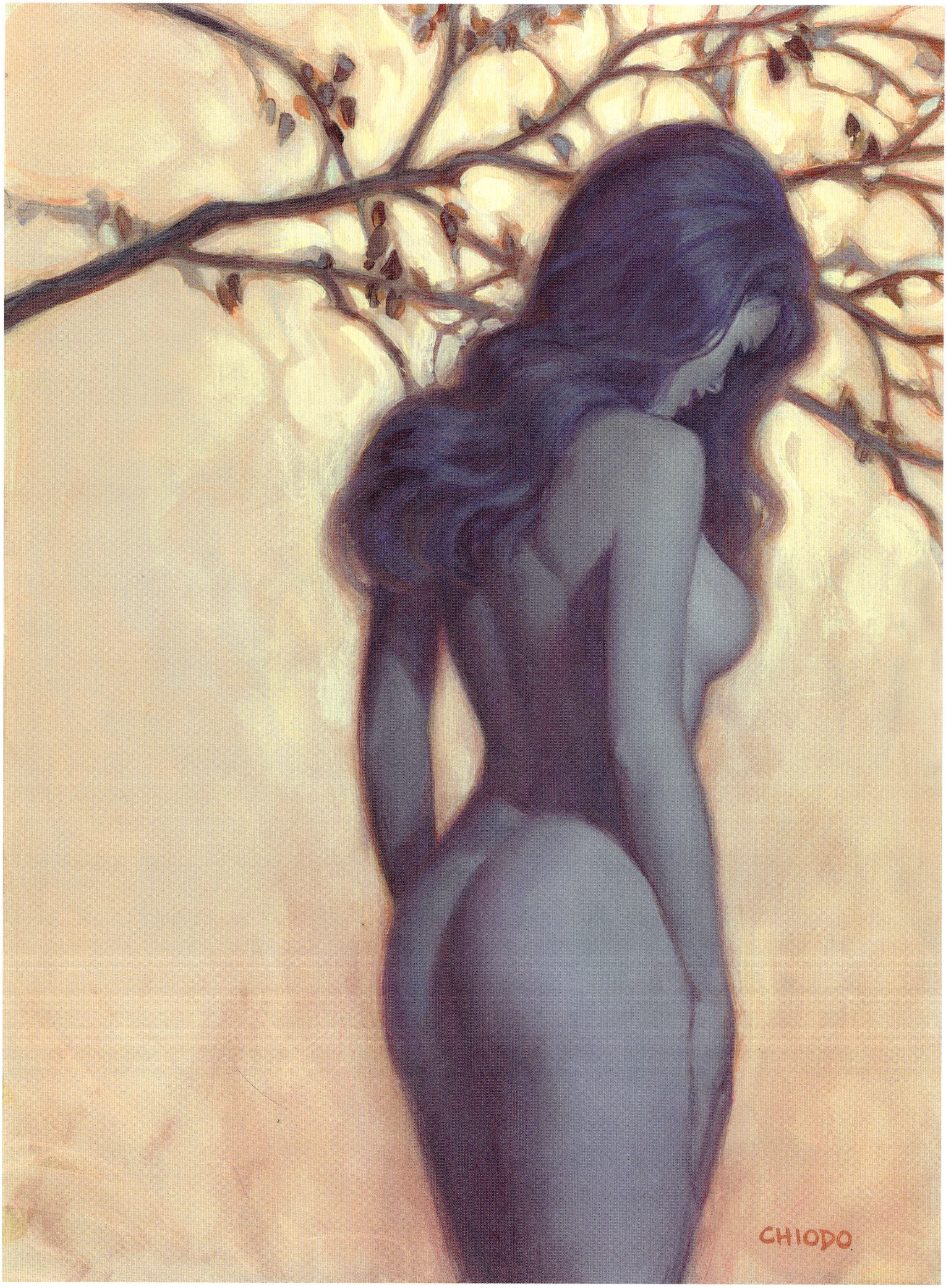
CHIODO

Left: Fall Leaves, 2002, acrylic and oil on masonite.
Below: Crossed Arms, 2002, oil on canvas.

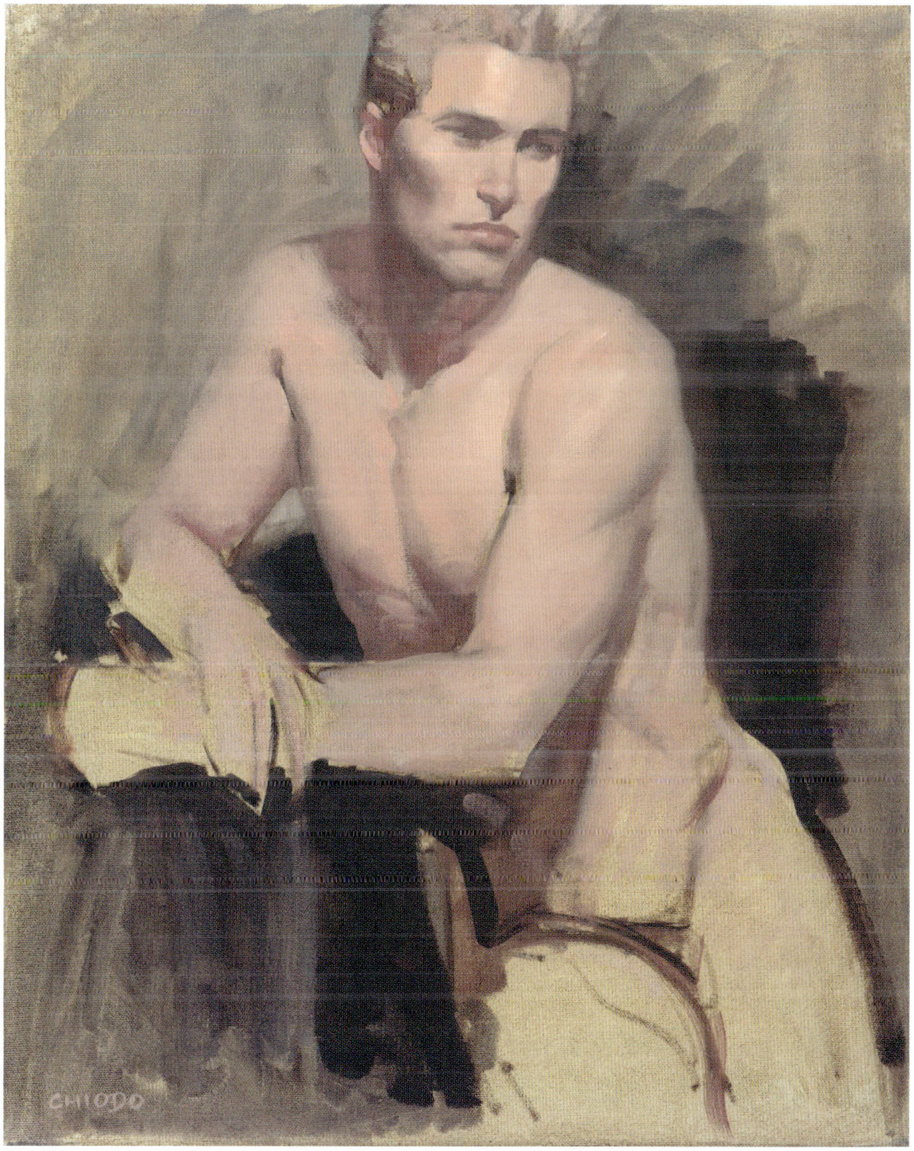

Below: Marsh, 2002, oil on canvas.
Right: Jason's Shades, 2001, oil on canvas.

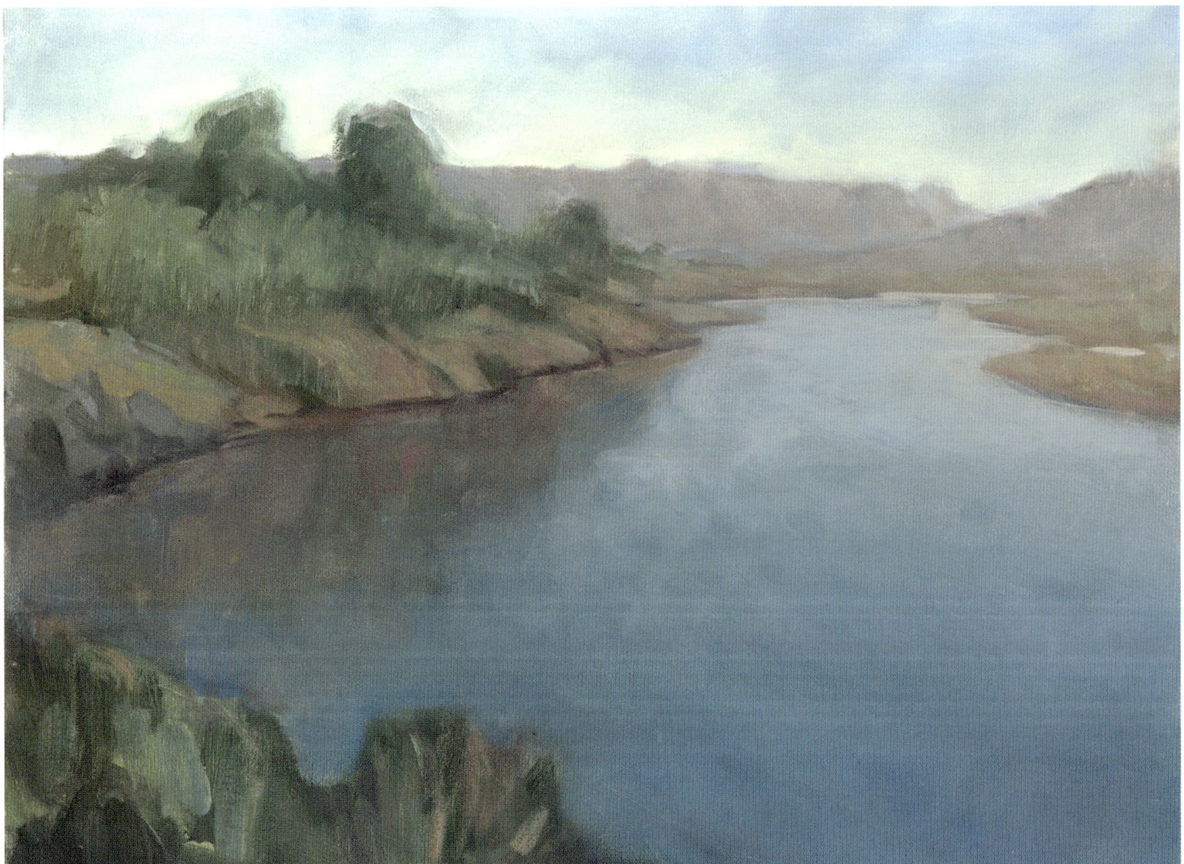

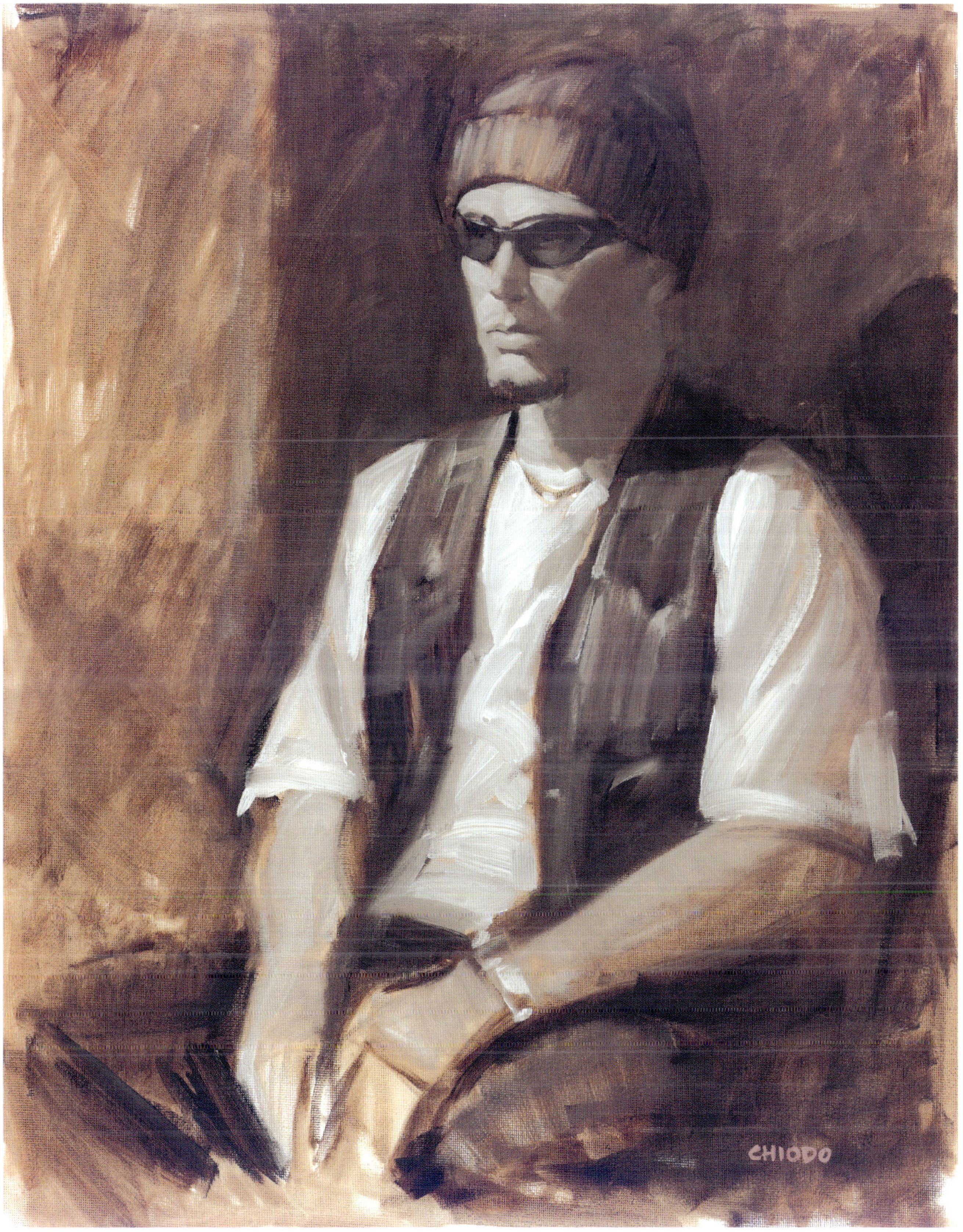
CHIODO

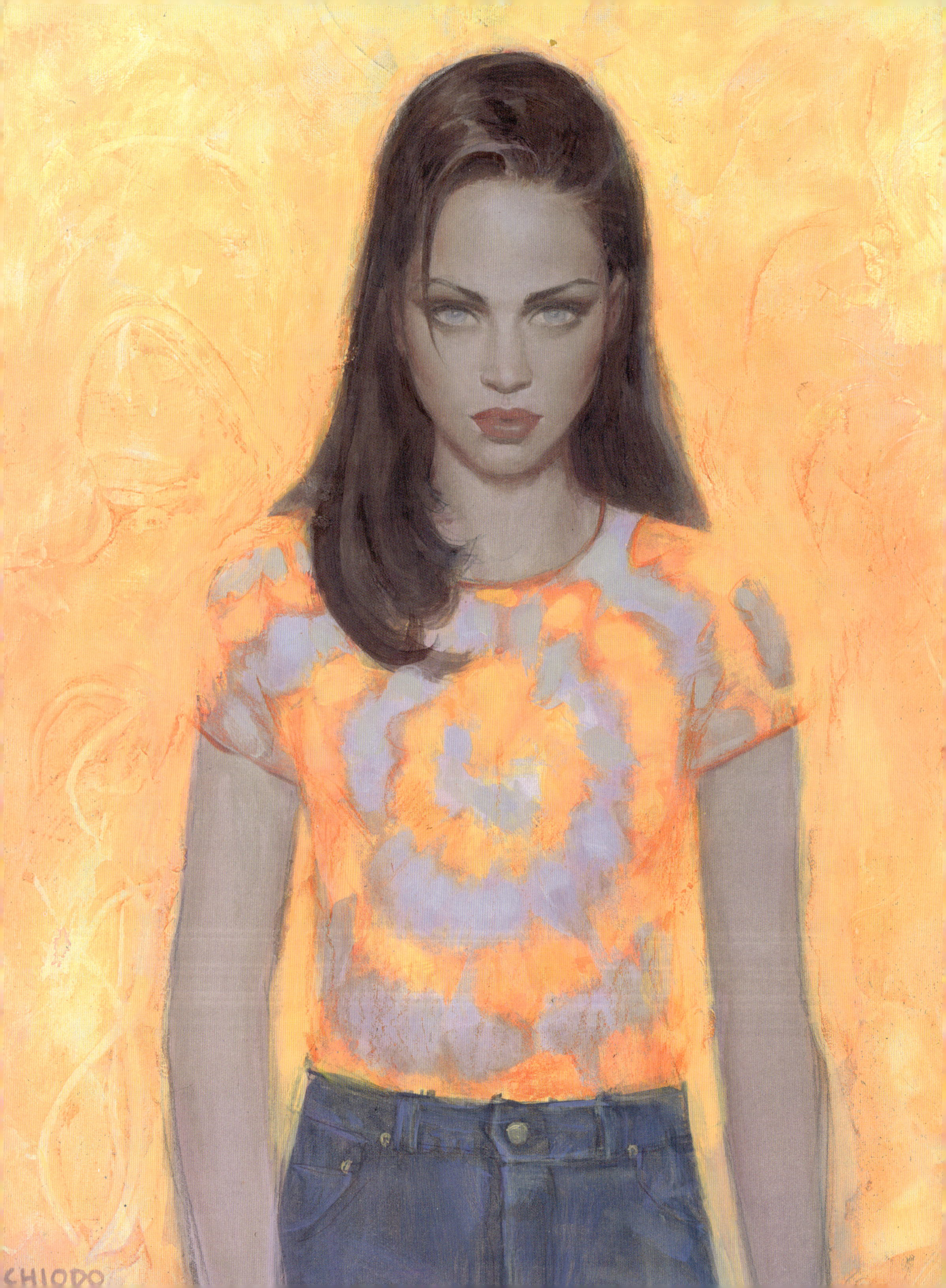
CHIODO

Left: Tie Dye, 2002, acrylic and oil on masonite.
Below: Toby, 2002, acrylic on board.

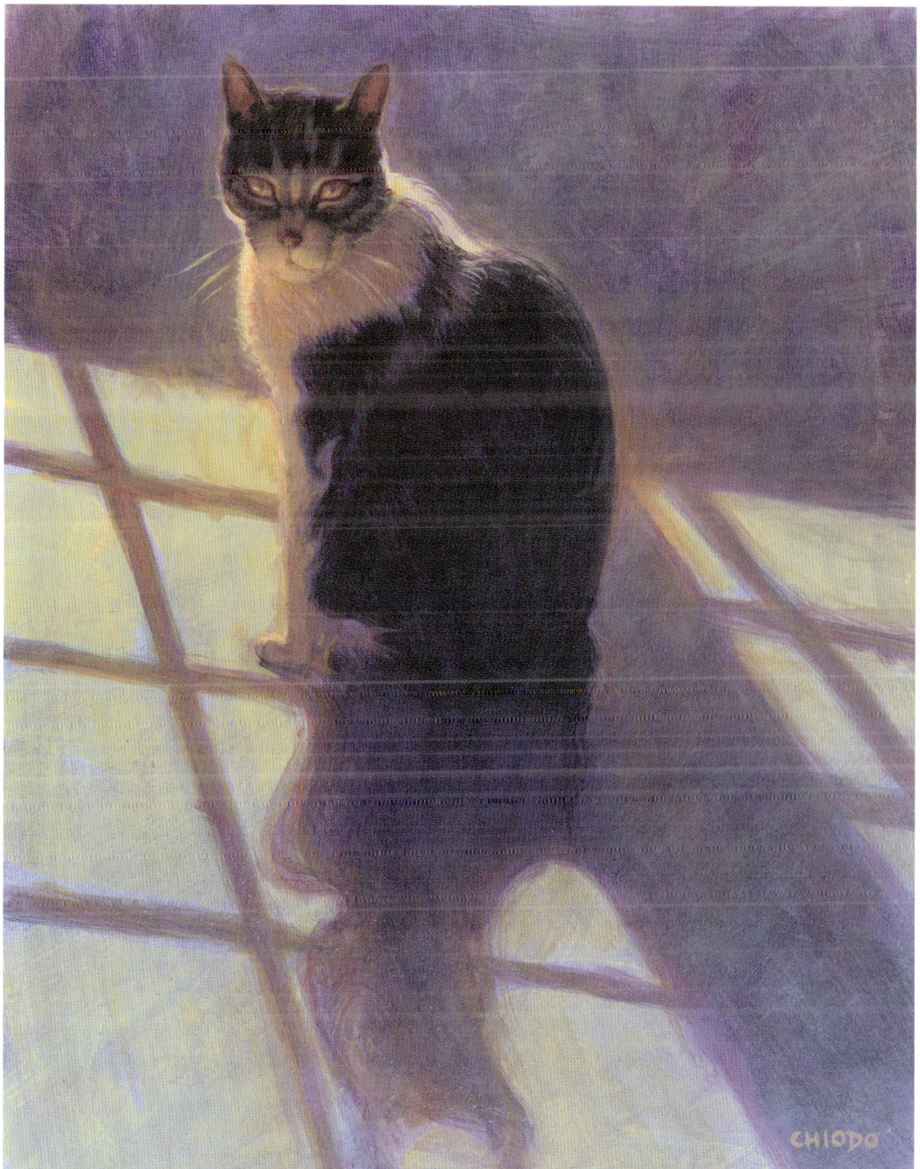

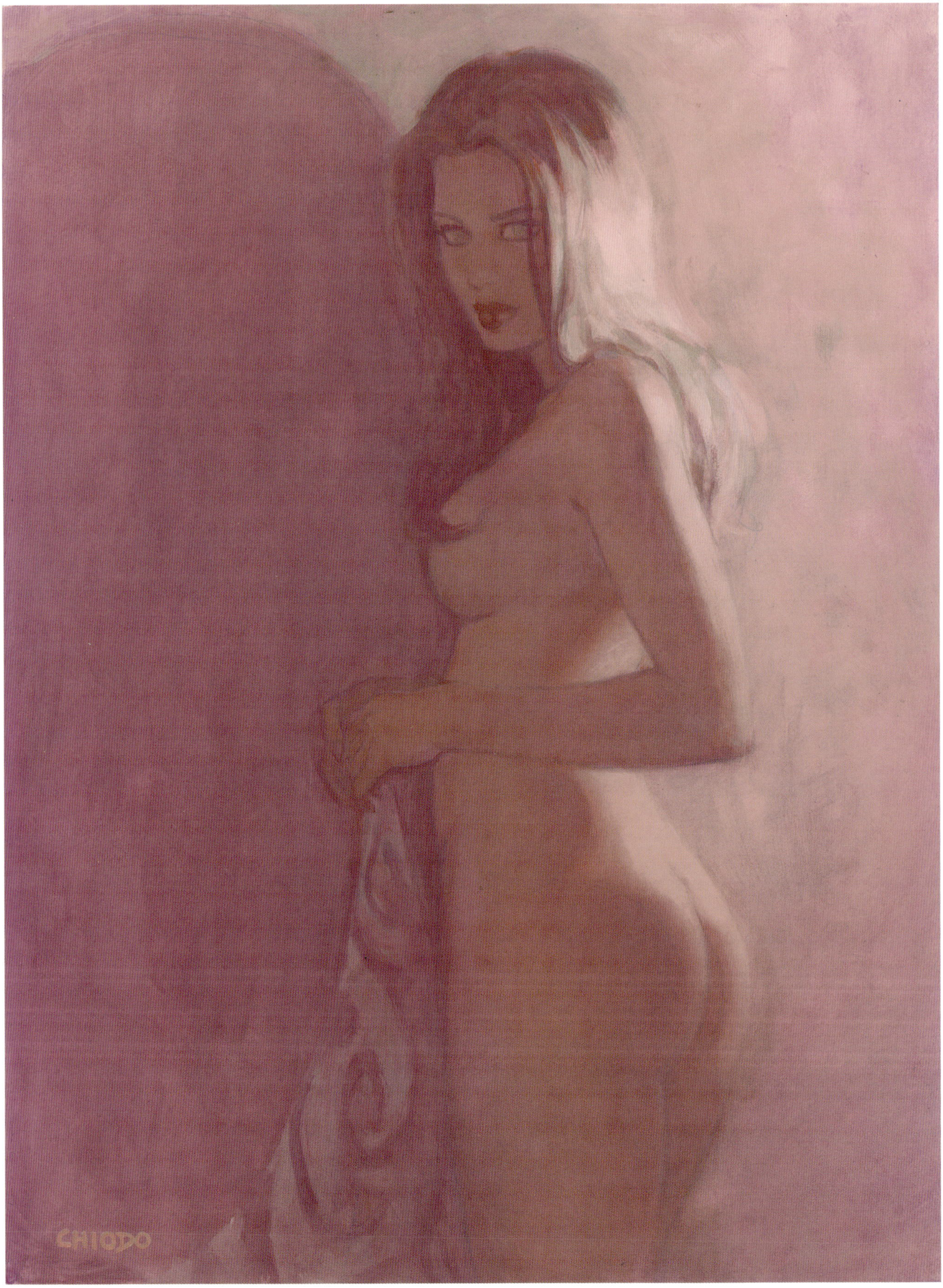

Robe, 2002, oil on masonite

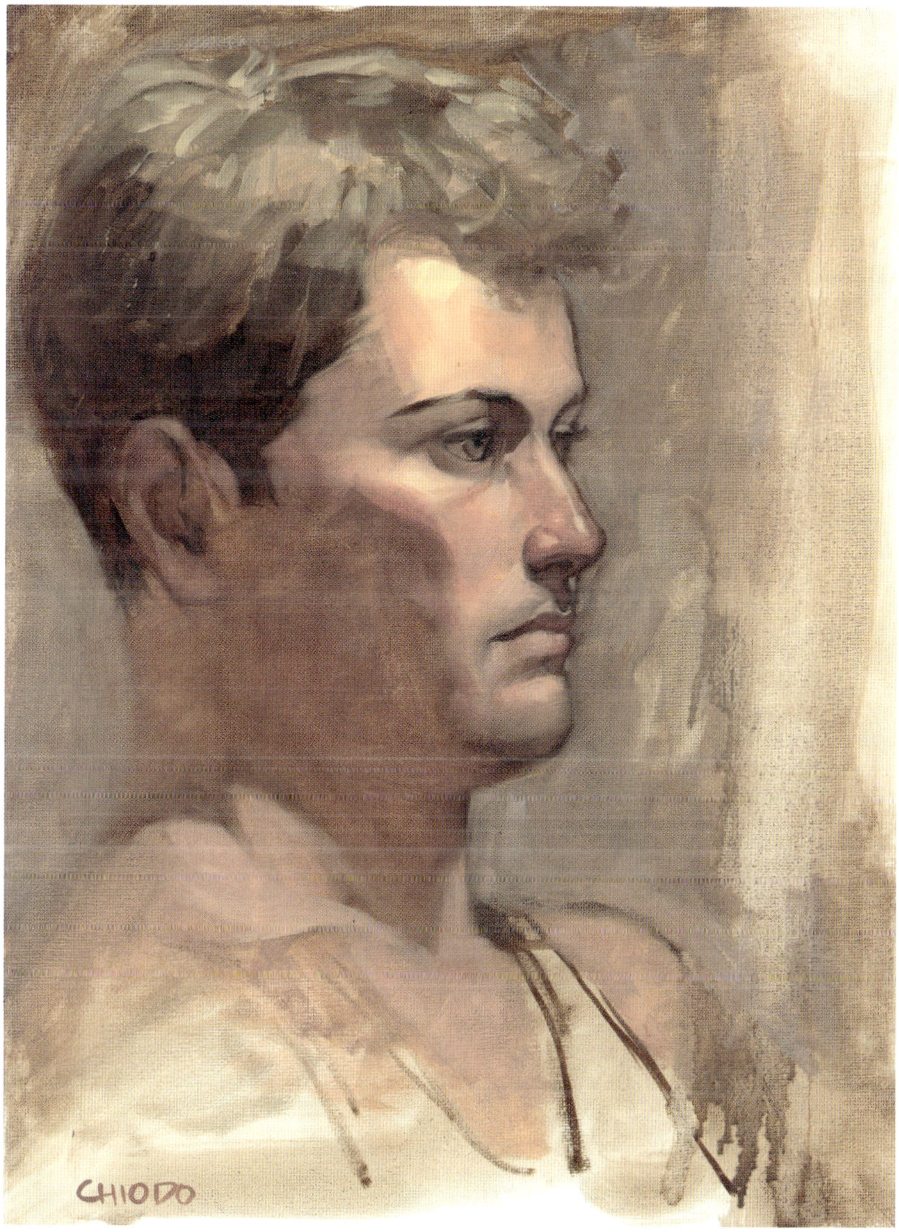

Profile with Stare, 2001, oil on canvas

Below: Pale Man, 2002, oil on canvas.
Right: Bruno, 2002, oil on canvas.

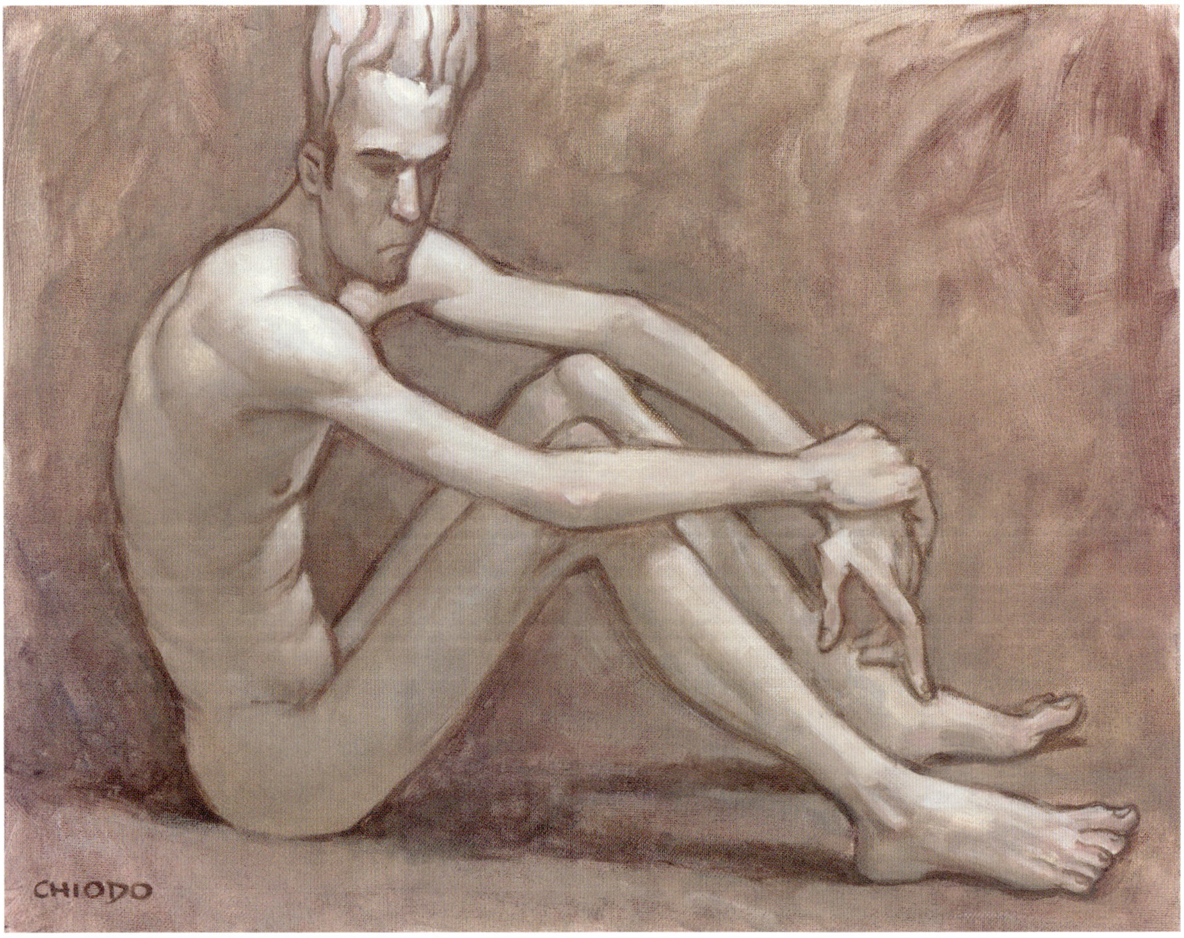

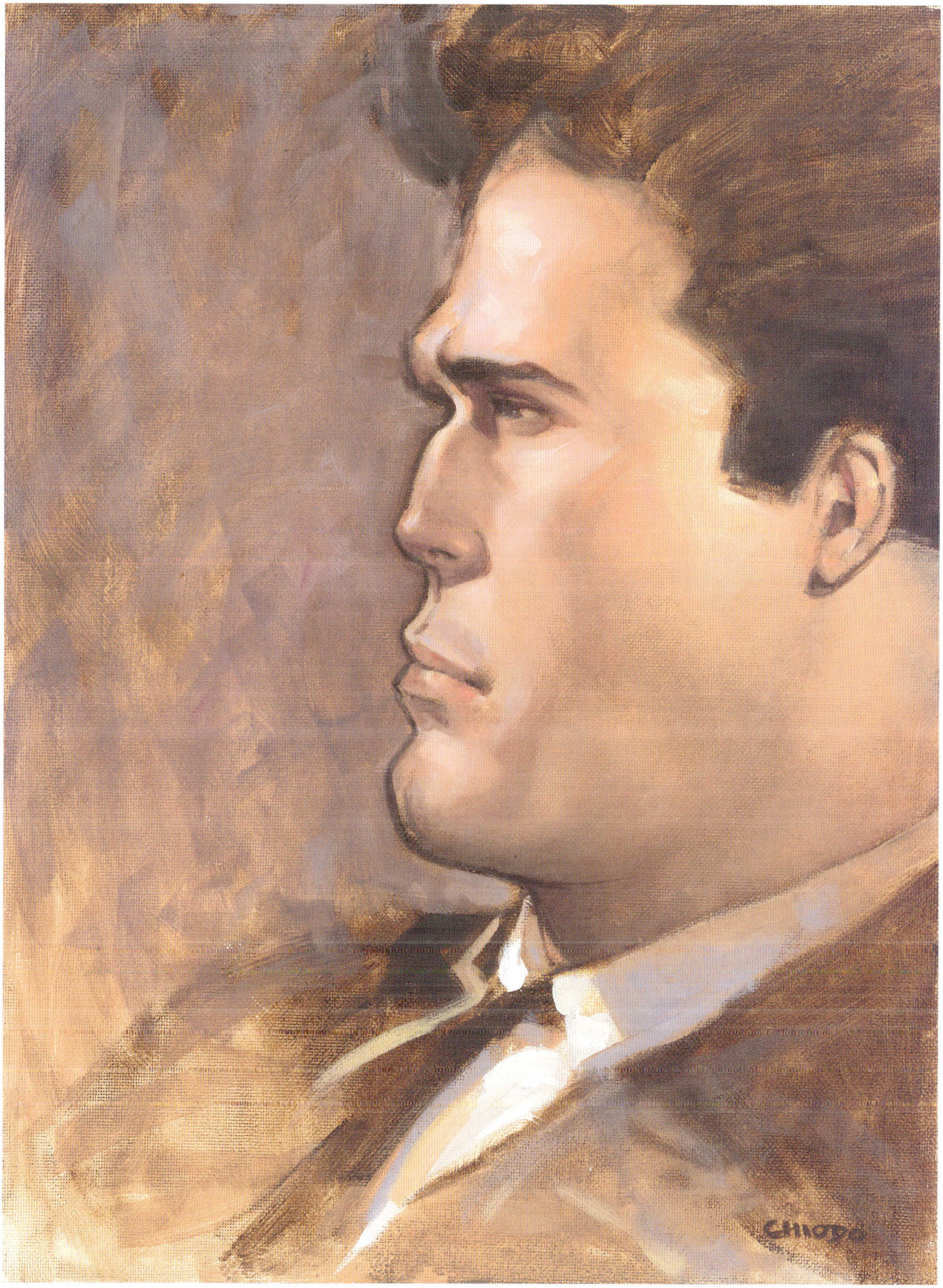
CHIODO

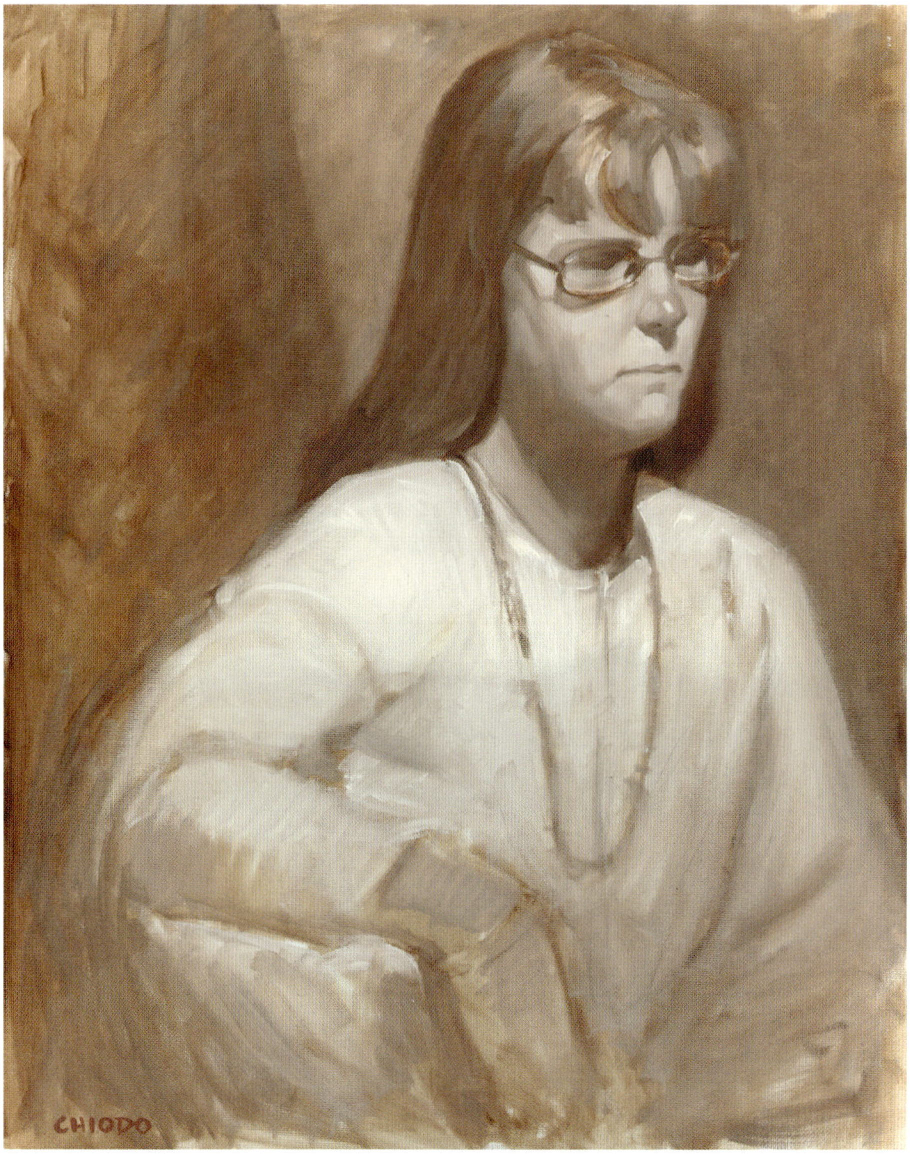

Above: Specks, 2001, oil on canvas.
Right: Jack, 2002, oil on canvas.

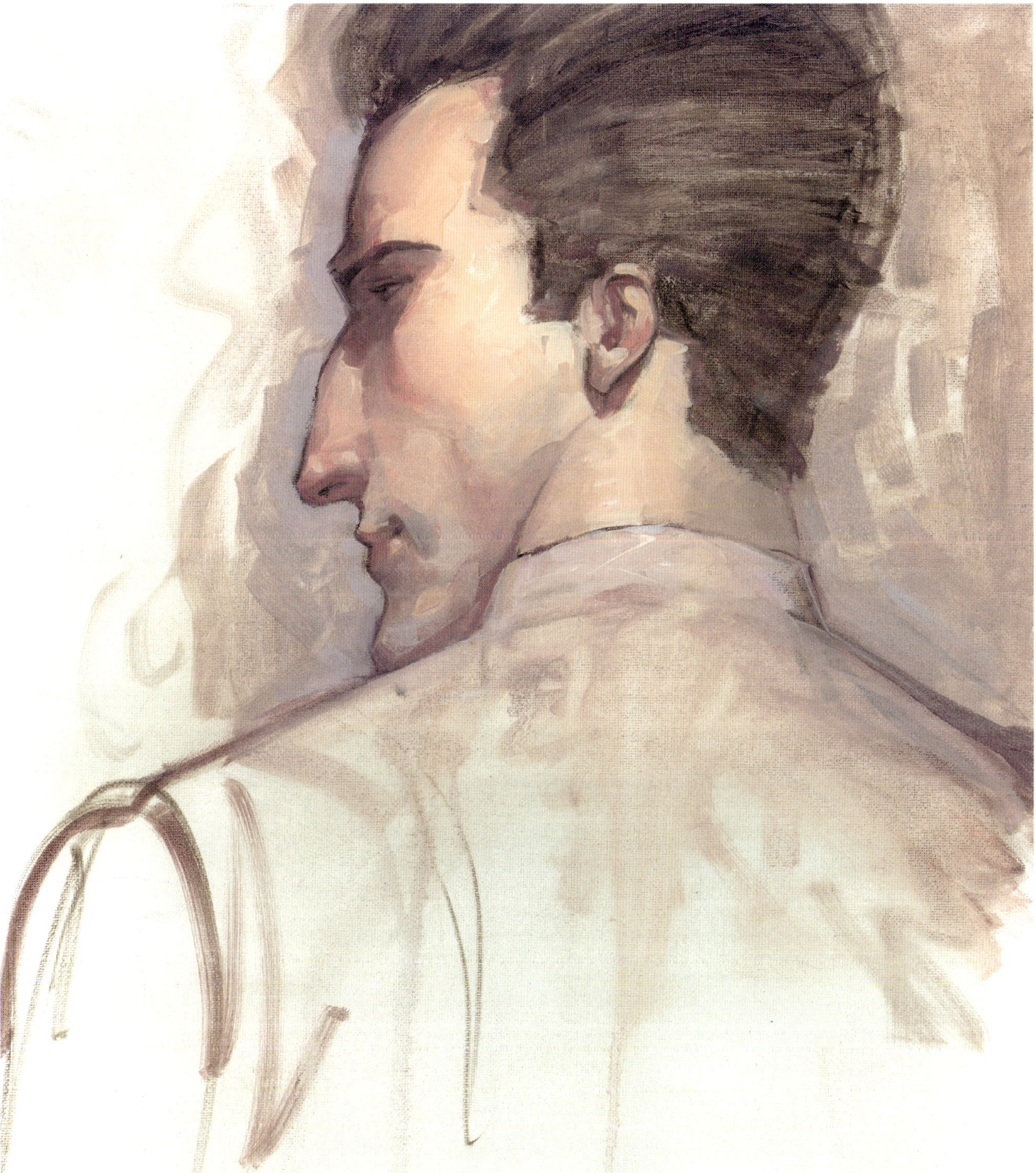

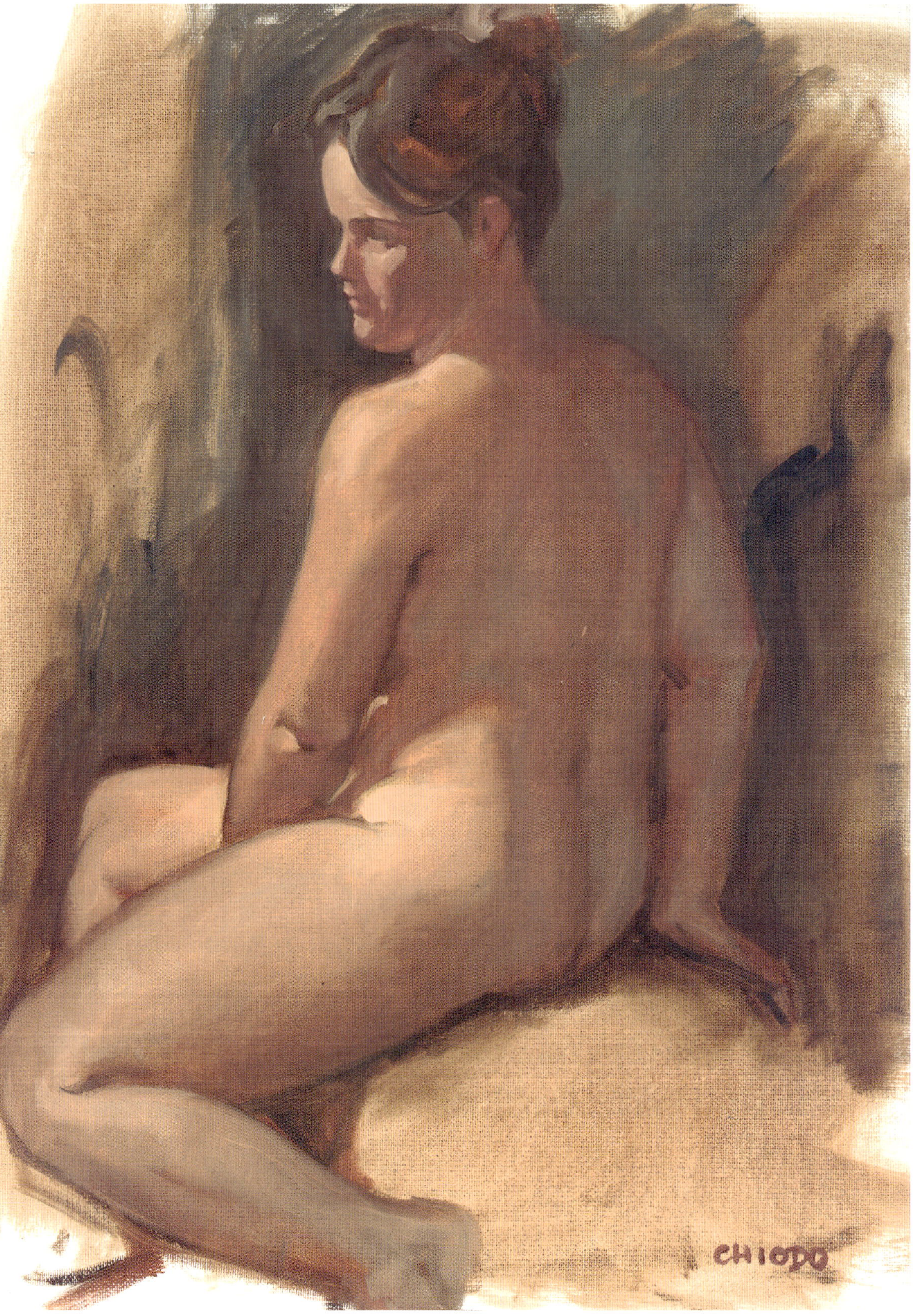
CHIODO

Left: Rubenesque, 2001, oil on canvas.
Below: Scarf, 2001, oil on canvas.

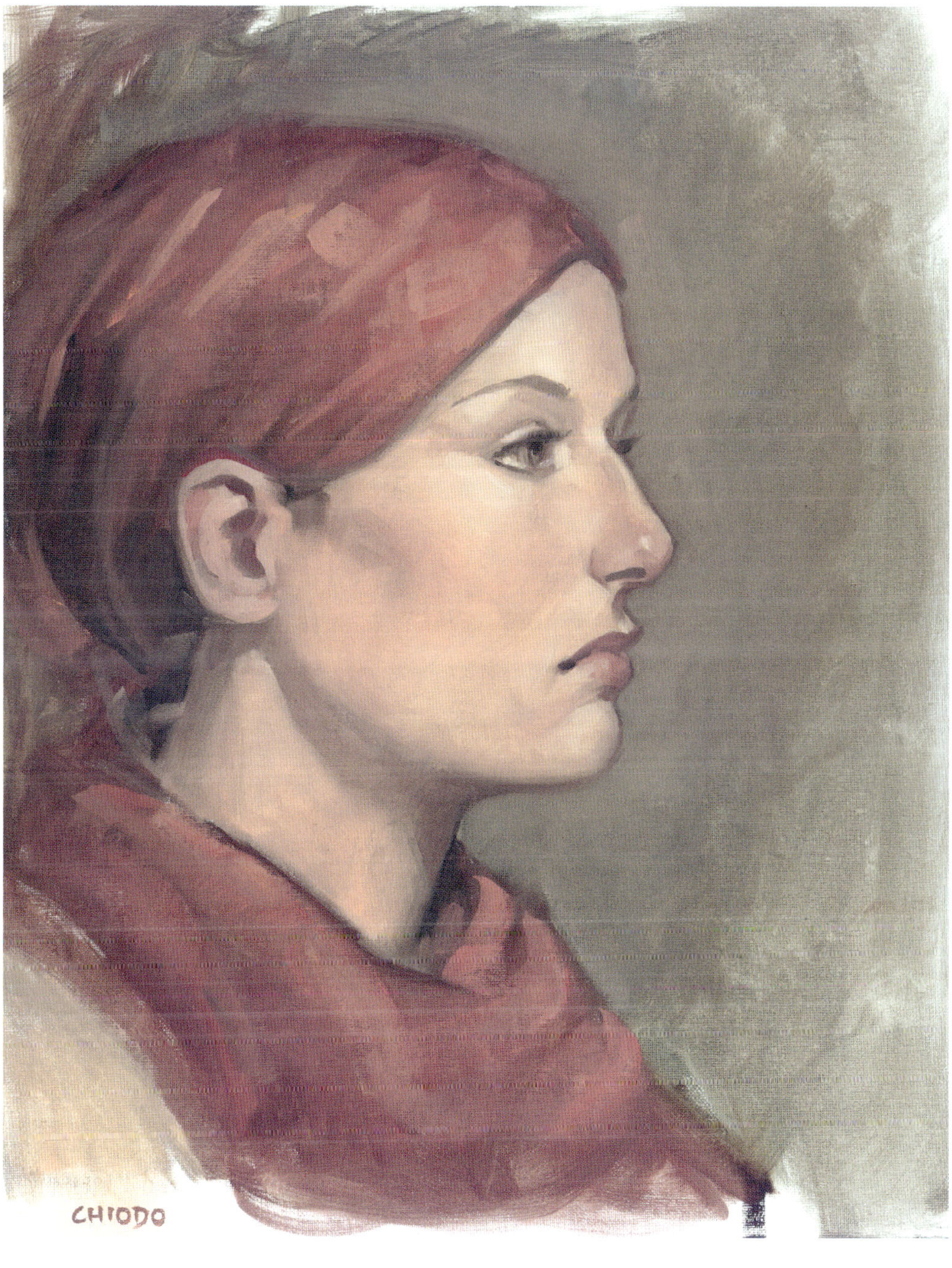

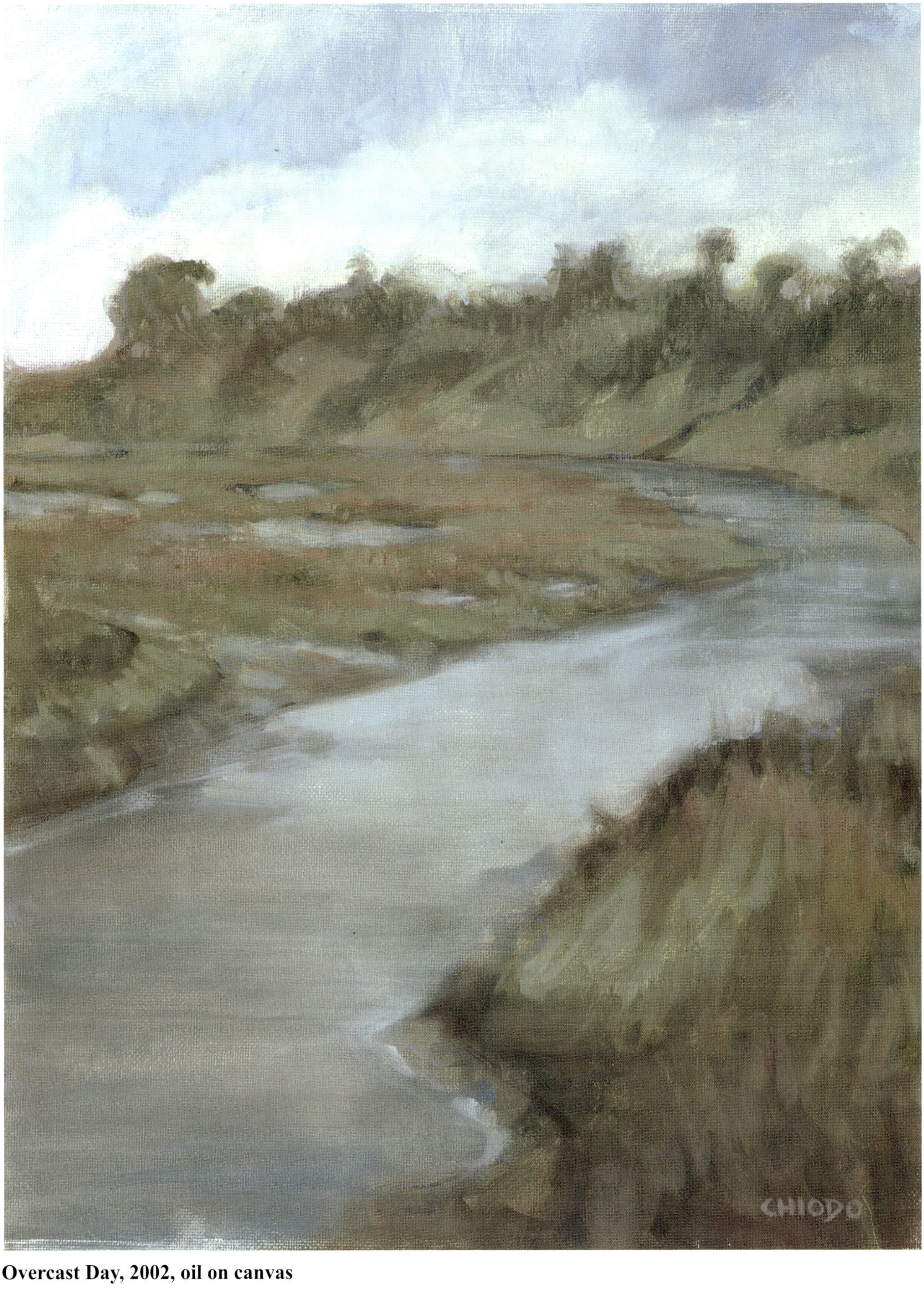

Overcast Day, 2002, oil on canvas

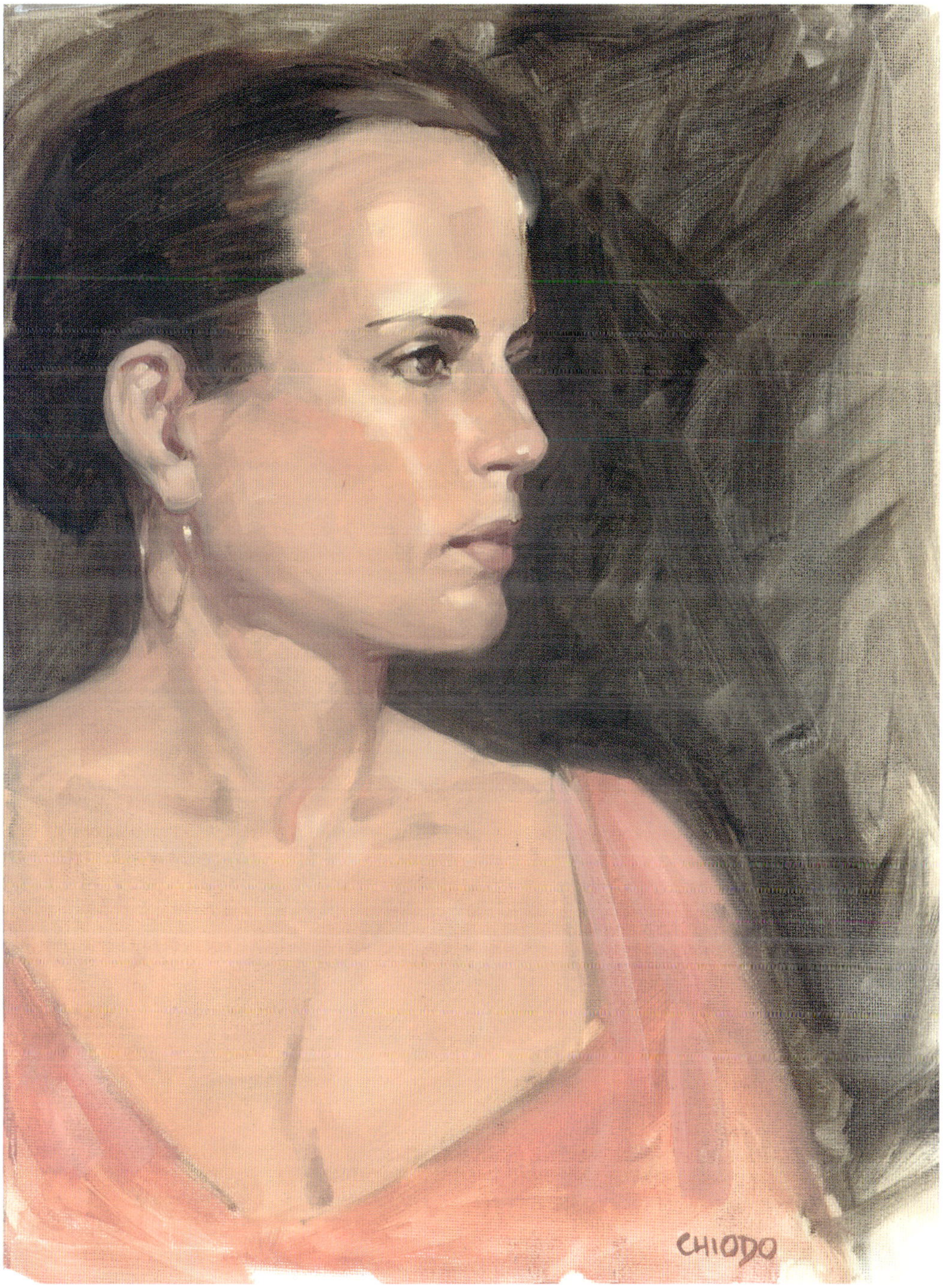

Pink Blouse, 2001, oil on canvas

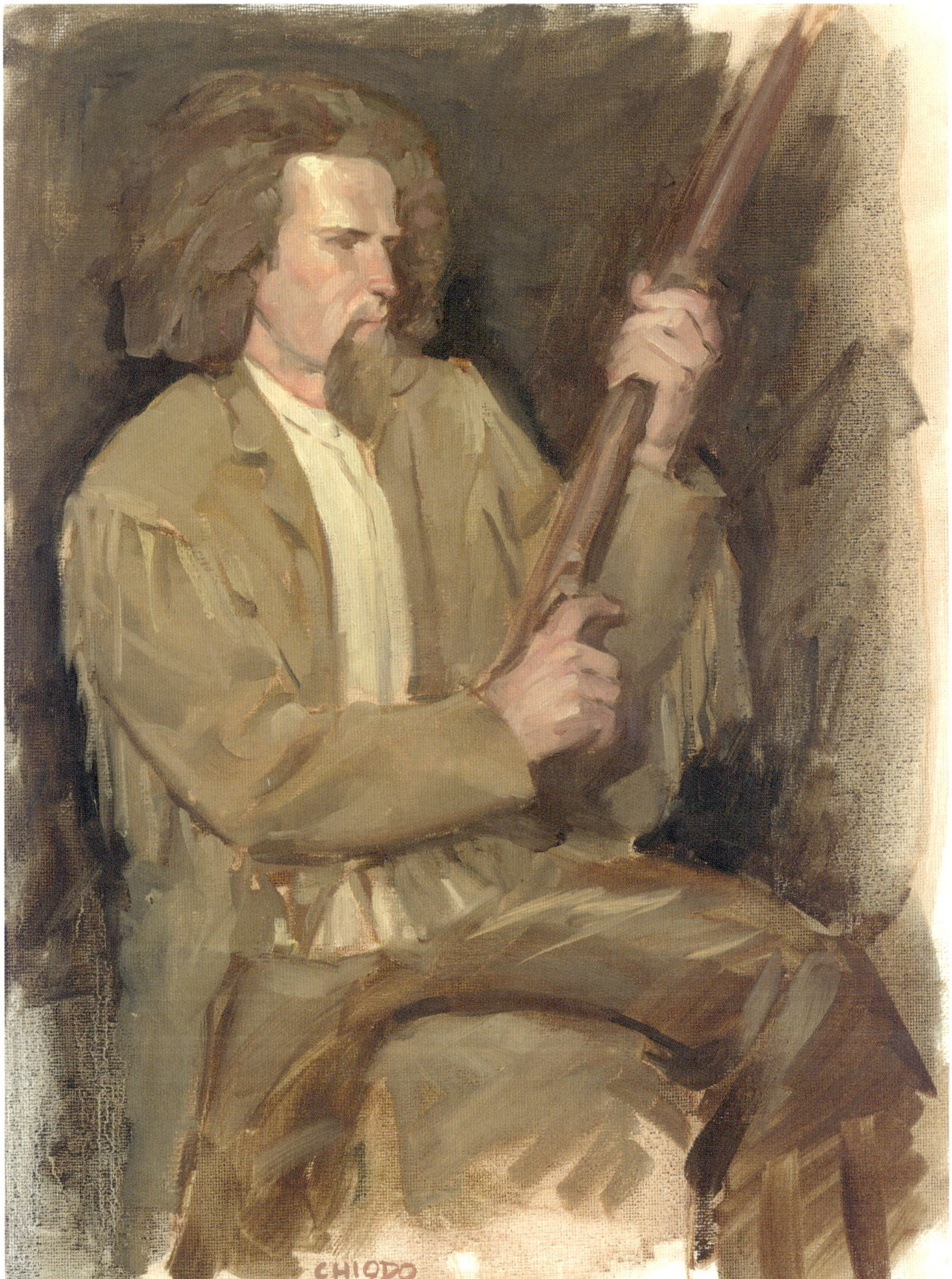

Mountain Man, 2001, oil on canvas

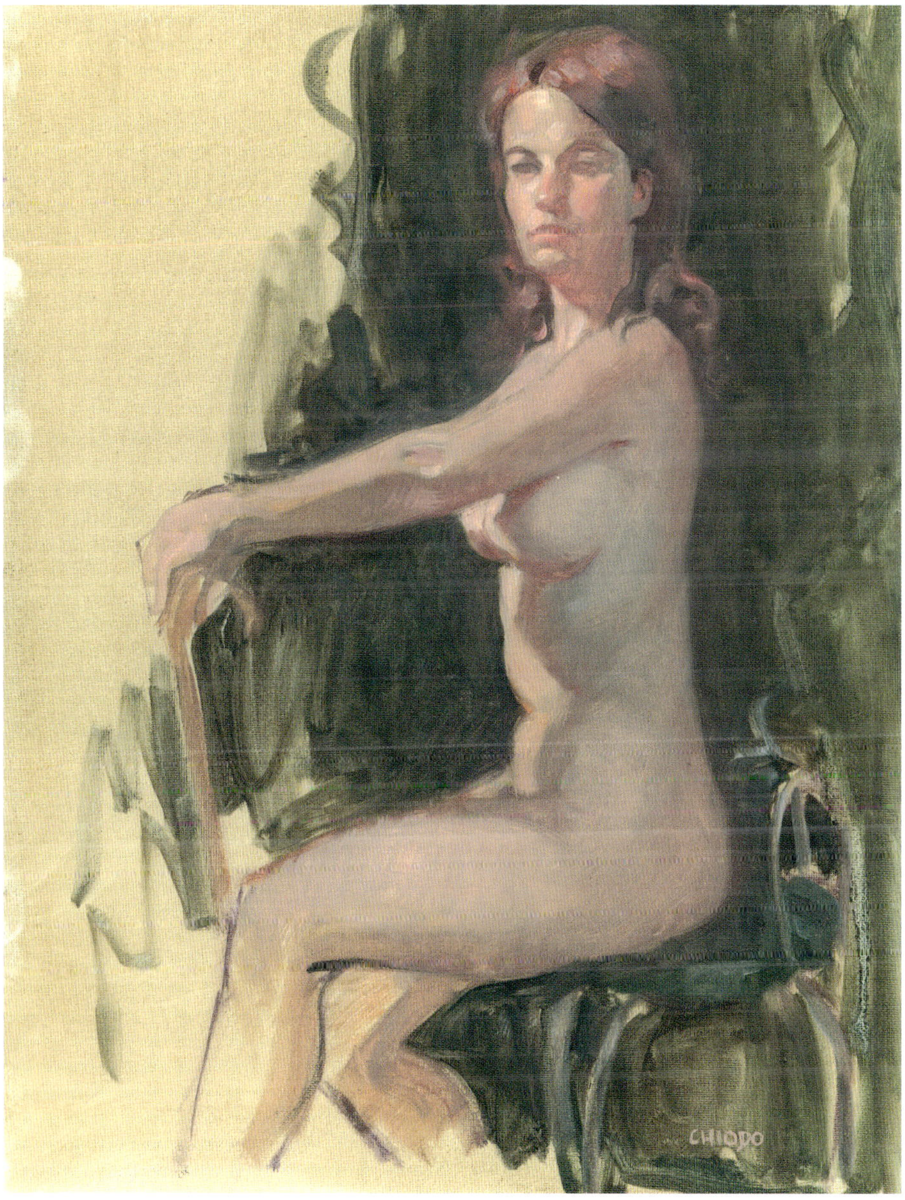

Red Hair, 2001, oil on canvas

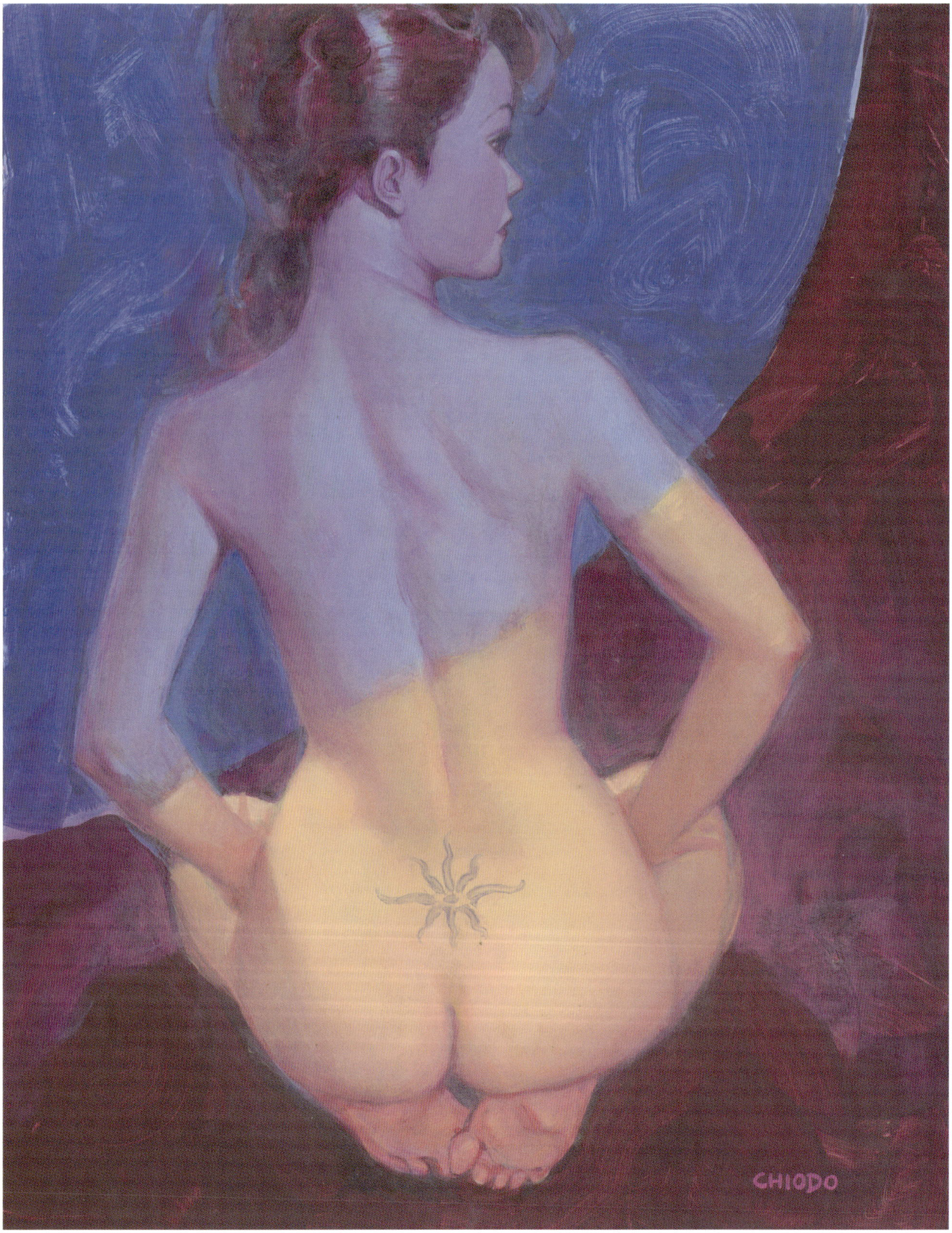

Tattoo, 2002, oil on masonite

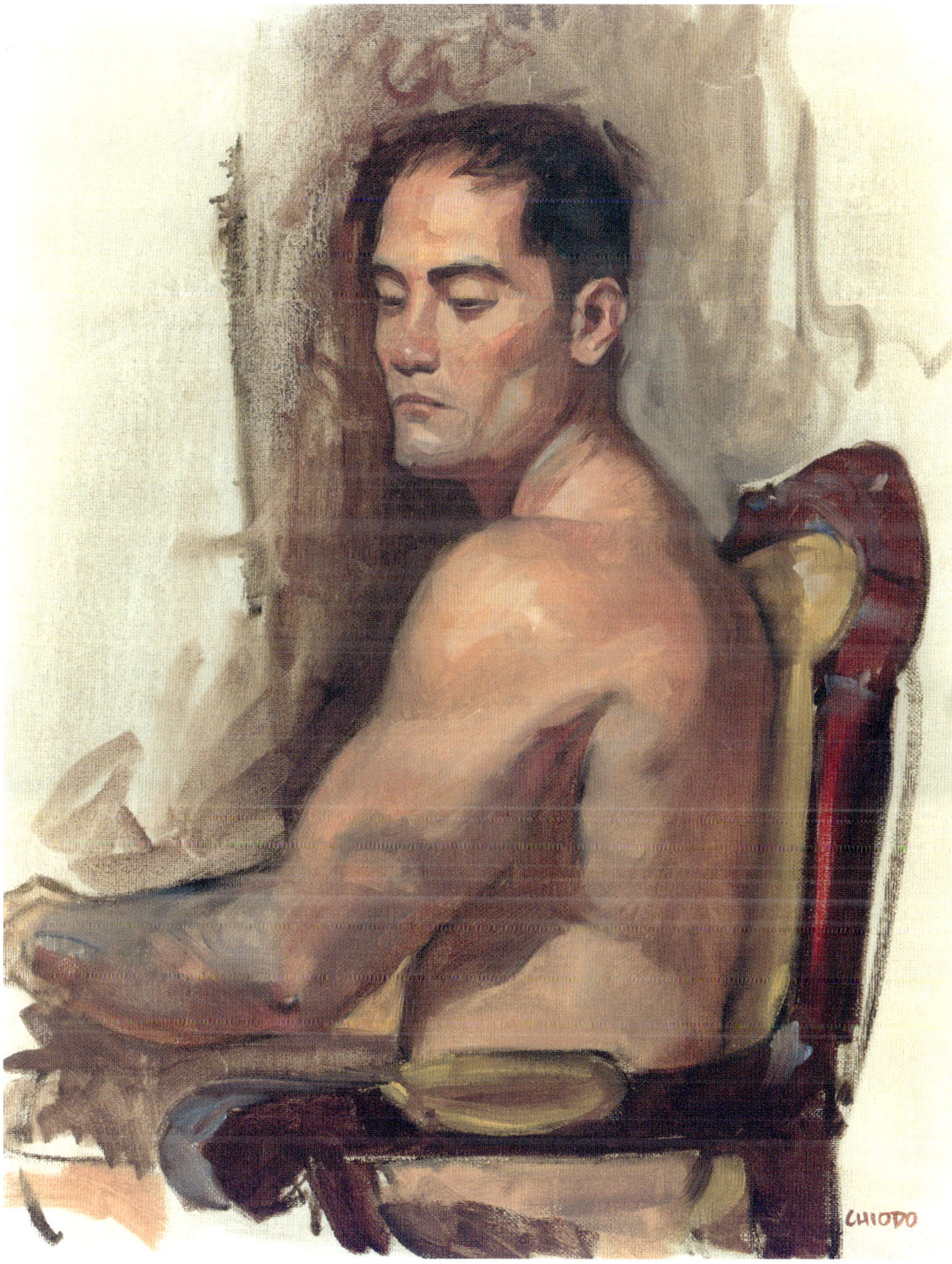

Red Chair, 2002, oil on canvas

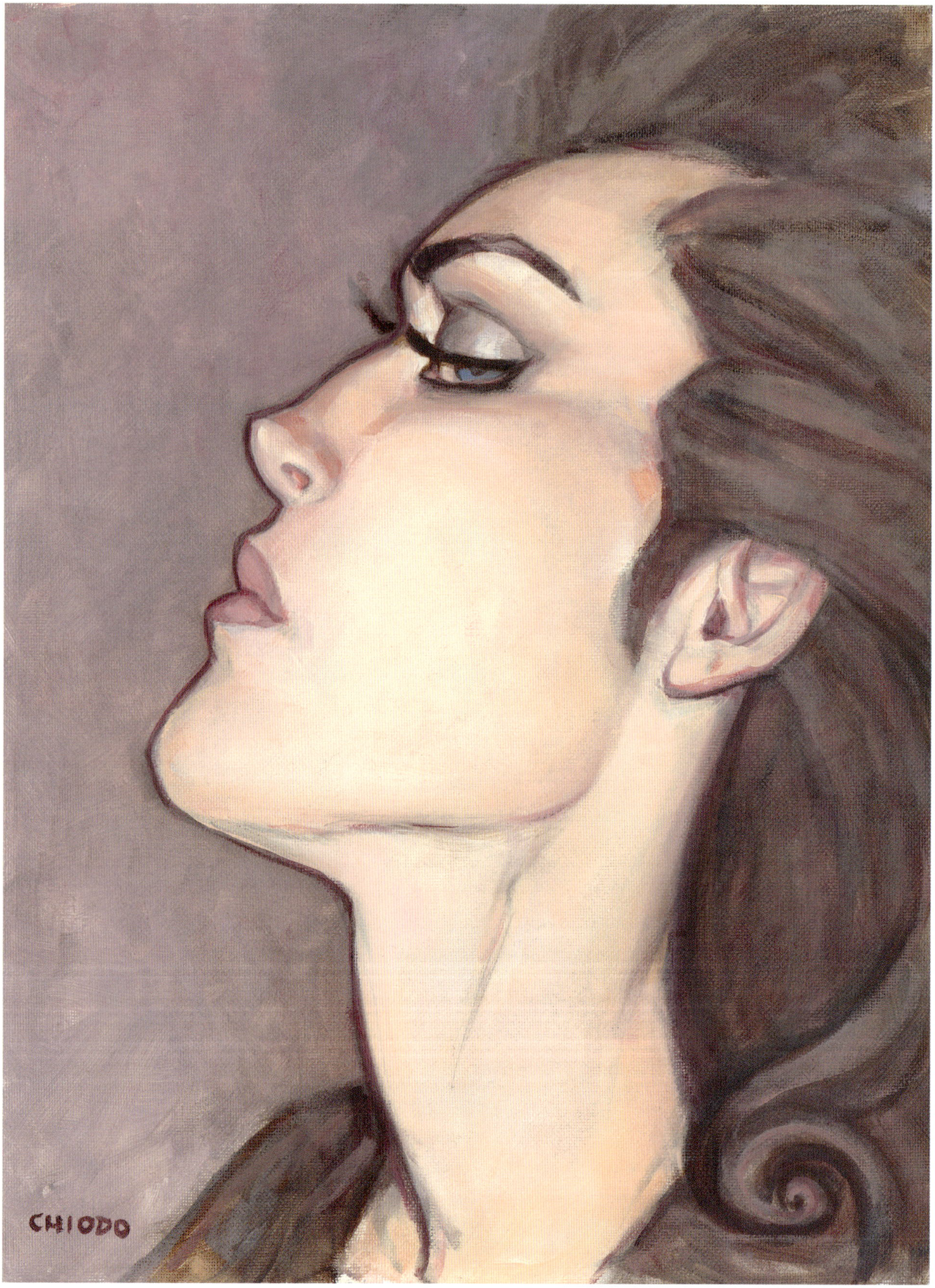

Sarcastic Glance, 2002, oil on canvas

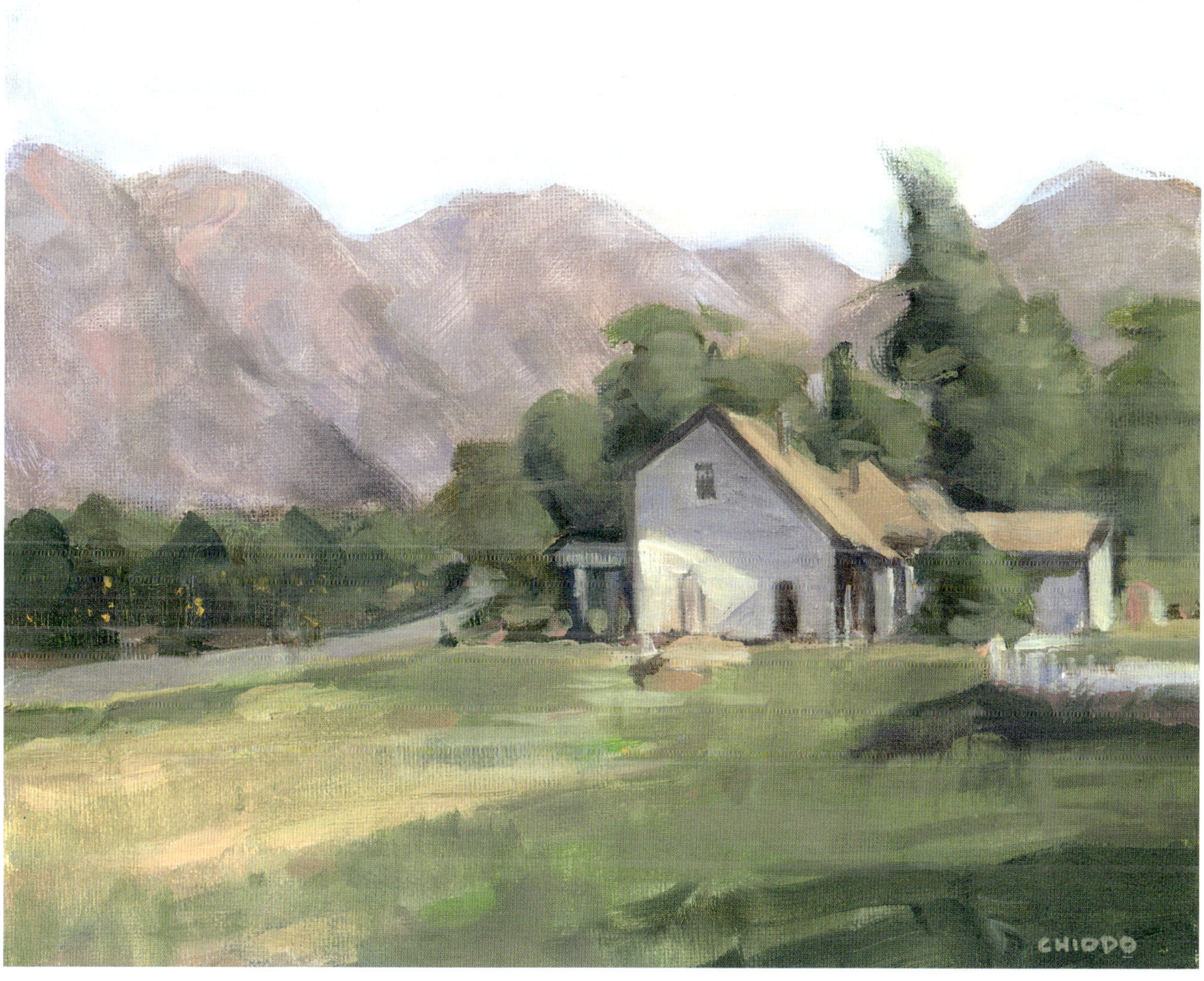

Farm House, 2002, oil on canvas

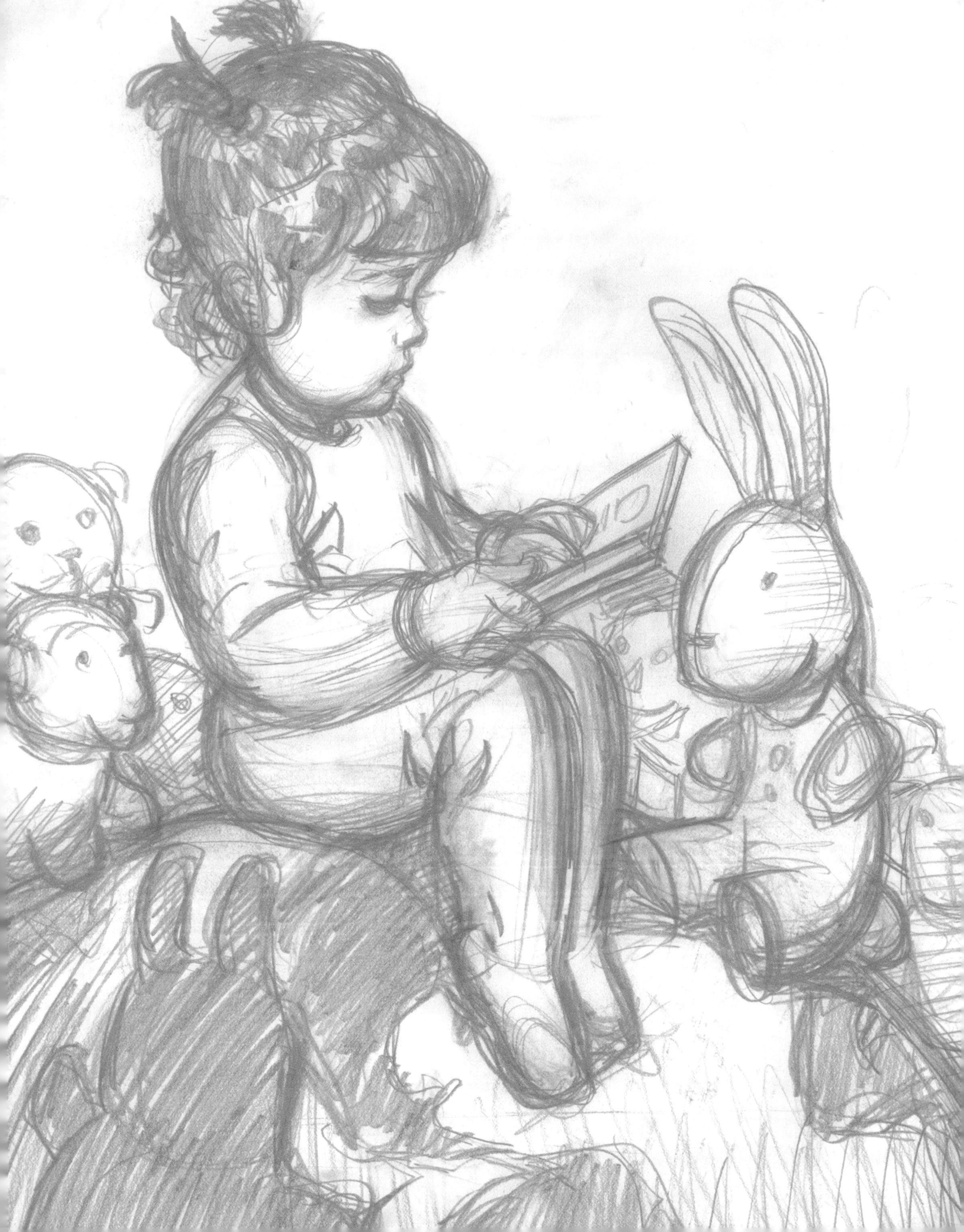

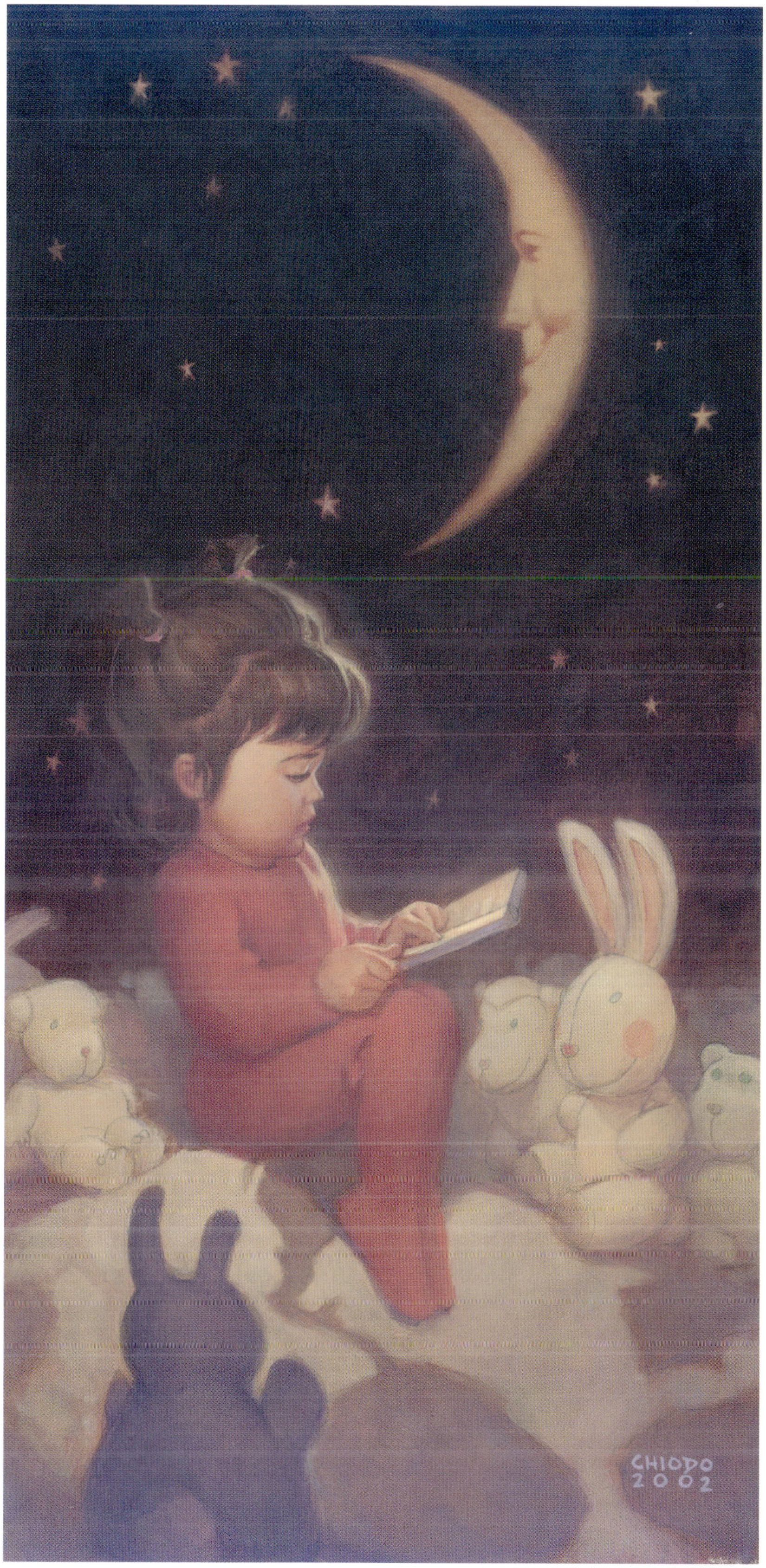

Left: Study, Nina's Book Party, 2002, pencil on paper. Right: Nina's Book Party, 2002, oil on masonite.

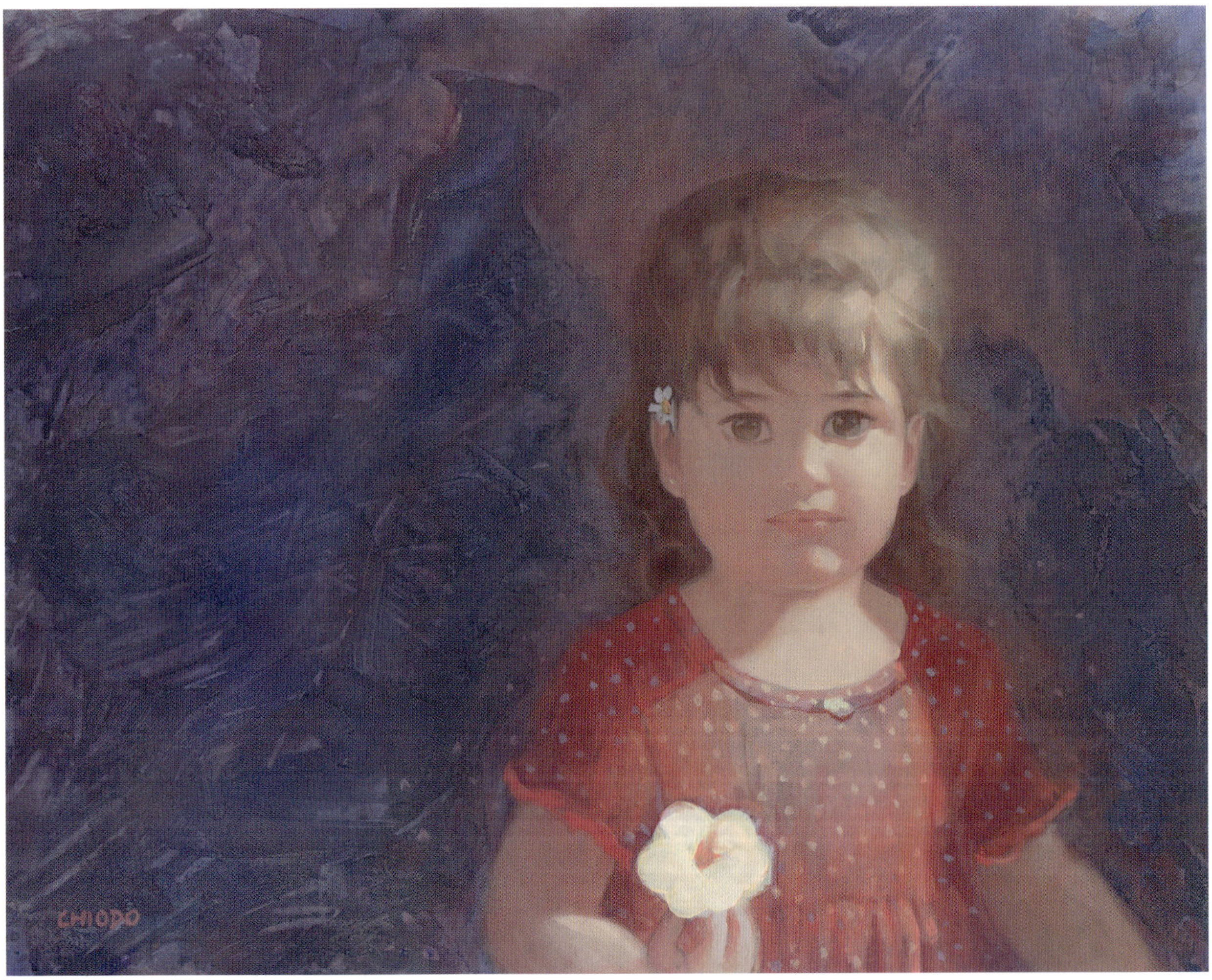

Nina's Gift, 2002, oil on masonite